The Web Conferencing Book

WITHDRAWN

D1520254

The Web Conferencing Book

- *Understand the technology.*
- *Choose the right vendors, software, and equipment.*
- *Start saving time and money today!*

By Sue Spielman & Liz Winfeld

AMACOM

American Management Association

New York • Atlanta • Brussels • Chicago • Mexico City • San Francisco
Shanghai • Tokyo • Toronto • Washington, D.C.

Special discounts on bulk quantities of AMACOM books are available to corporations, professional associations, and other organizations. For details, contact Special Sales Department, AMACOM, a division of American Management Association
1601 Broadway, New York, NY 10019.
Tel.: 212-903-8316. Fax: 212-903-8083.
Web site: www.amanet.org

This publication is designed to provide accurate and authoritative information in regard to the subject matter covered. It is sold with the understanding that the publisher is not engaged in rendering legal, accounting, or other professional service. If legal advice or other expert assistance is required, the services of a competent professional person should be sought.

Library of Congress Cataloging-in-Publication Data

Spielman, Sue.
 The Web conferencing book : understand the technology, choose the right vendors, software, and equipment. start saving time and money today! / by Sue Spielman & Liz Winfeld.
         p. cm.
Includes bibliographical references and index.
   ISBN 0-8144-7174-9
 1. Internet. 2. Computer conferencing. I. Winfeld, Liz. II. Title.

TK5105.875.I57S675 2003
004.67'8--dc21

                                                                2003056003

Printing number

10 9 8 7 6 5 4 3 2 1

CONTENTS

ACKNOWLEDGMENTS

The authors would like to acknowledge the time and effort given this project by people throughout the web conferencing world: Billy Sanez and Nita Miller at HP, Julie Blake and Jake Sorofman at eRoom, Paul Joyal and Elisabeth Hershman at Genesys, Stacy Kirincic at Intercall, Katy Rogers and Jennifer Chisholm of Interwise, Tom Patterson at Spartacom, Kent Kappen at PlaceWare, Beth Warren of WorkWorlds, Ellen Slaby at Centra, Elyse Mintz at Colorgraphic, and Praful Shah and Colin Smith of WebEx.

The authors thank Bev and Sid Winfeld for proofreading the manuscript before its submission, despite their trepidation about reading techie stuff. And also Amy and Les Spielman, just for being them.

Finally, Sue and Liz would like to thank Jacquie Flynn, our acquisitions editor at AMACOM, who's worked with us before . . . but did it again anyway.

PREFACE

Let's say Liz runs a consulting business. And actually, we can say this with a great deal of confidence because Liz does, indeed, run a consulting business. The primary mission of her business is developing and delivering diversity education in really small to really big companies, corporations, universities, non-profits, and what have you. Hers is decidedly a warm and fuzzy, human-focus endeavor; one that uses technology to an extent to be sure, but not one that is dependent upon it. In fact, Liz is sure she could go an entire week without checking her email and without losing her sanity if she did. The same cannot be said for Sue. Sue's a software engineer.

Sue also runs her own business, but hers is a software engineering consulting business and as such is very much involved in, and involved with, computer technology. She builds software for companies of all sizes who do all sorts of things. Sue is a high-level engineer, a woman able to operate in this world at the architectural level. She's an anomaly in the industry for that reason because, as recent studies demonstrate, young women are still not being encouraged to go into technical or computer fields. And there's an aspect of social injustice that Liz would love to discuss more, but we digress.

Sue is the type of person who takes to technology on an intuitive level, in very much the same way that our dogs just know that rubber balls are good things very much meant to be trifled with. Technology holds no aura of mystery for Sue; she just gets it. She can pick up a book about any aspect of software, read it, and immediately understand and begin to use it. Liz, on the other hand, has an excellent grasp of how to turn her PC on and off.

Within this authoring partnership, therefore, we have an equitable representation of the two types of people currently occupying the planet, at least in so far as computer use for work and leisure is concerned. One contributor totally gets it and is completely comfortable with all the new toys evolving and coming down the pike; the other contributor firmly believes that while she may have been born forty years too late, she has the capacity to research, dabble, and learn.

How This Book Came About

Over the last year or so, many things have conspired to make the technological advances of the Internet more important to a great number of people. For example, in a business context for a trainer like Liz, the economic downturn that started in late Q2 of 2001, followed closely by the horrific events of September that year, led not only to a hesitancy of people to travel if they really didn't absolutely have to, but also to a literal inability to engage in business travel because the people in charge said, "There isn't going to be any travel for a while. A long while." And in a personal, or home use, context, those same events and realities caused people to become very creative about how they keep in touch and interact with family and friends.

So as 2001 turned into 2002, Liz quickly realized she had a significant business problem: her inability to get in front of her clients face-to-face. That's when Sue mentioned web conferencing as a possible solution to her growing conundrum. It's not that Sue's mere mention of web conferencing technology solved all of Liz' problems, unfortunately; only the winning Powerball numbers would do that. But it represented an avenue of exploration that she'd not previously thought of as possible for a small business like hers to implement and use profitably. Liz was intrigued, to say the least, and wanted to know more.

So Liz went out looking for a book about web conferencing technologies for home and business—what they are, how they work, how to set them up, how to best leverage them, how to make money or just have fun with them . . . and she didn't find a single one. Video conferencing? Plenty of books out there. Strategies about how to best leverage, design, and deliver the content you present over the web? Tons of tomes to choose from. Books about the philosophical righteousness and economic imperatives of doing remotely what was once only done in person? A virtual (pardon the pun) library of literature to choose from. But a book about web conferencing specifically that lays out the available vendors and their strategies for delivering this technology; that tells you what applications work best and how, that explains the features and user interfaces of salient products, that tells you what they require from an equipment standpoint and how to set it all up, that tells you what all this is going to cost you? Nothing. Nada. Nil. Zip. Zero. Until now.

We were frankly amazed that there wasn't a single book out there in the world already that explained all this, or even that such ground-level information was not available on the websites of, or via links from many, if not all, of the vendors who operate in this space. Their websites are informative, no doubt, but not highly explanatory.

Not Everything About the Web Is on the Web

Informative is not the same as *explanatory,* and as we said, the websites of the vendors you might visit to see if you want to investigate using their products are informative, but they don't explain things very well to the level necessary, in our opinion, for the vast majority of people who populate the Web. Liz is the non-technologist who is interested in actually using web conferencing. That makes her the perfect stand-in for the vast majority of readers. When you're done reading this book you, like Liz, will understand how the technology works and will be able to use it effectively.

So, the book you hold in your hands now bridges the gap between "information" and "explanation" when it comes to web conferencing. After reading it, you'll know as much as Sue does about it, which in itself will be enough to impress people at parties. Also, you'll have the same comfort and command level with it all as Liz does, thereby in fact giving you the option of conferencing into those parties and not having to shower or dress or eat dry chicken wings.

Whether you need or want to use web conferencing to run your business, better manage remote workforces or projects, share documents and data with peers, interact with clients in different time zones or who are simply hard to pin down, deliver training to your workforce in myriad locations or . . . if you are just a home PC user who would like to have discussions with far flung family (and mute them without them knowing when they aggravate you), show off your new golf clubs and lie about your handicap to buddies back home, or just get pictures of your grandkids to hang or your ex to burn, web conferencing is an affordable, easy-to-use, accessible technology you must become familiar with.

And we're just the women to show you how.

The Web
Conferencing Book

Unraveling Web Conferencing— What It's Really Made of, What You Can Do with It

The really good news for you, the user, about web conferencing technologies and products is that they can do a lot that business and home users will, and do, find inordinately valuable, innovative, creative, cost-effective, and just plain fun. The bad news about web conferencing technologies and products for you, the user, is that you can only do what business and home users would find inordinately valuable, innovative, creative, cost-effective, and just plain fun if you really understand and are familiar with the technology and products. Without some sort of logical and complete guide, many people will never know how useful web conferencing can be; or even if they've gotten a whiff of that, they won't know how to get the most out of their interest and investment in it.

Web conferencing in today's world is like those studies that maintain that the average person uses only 6 percent of their available brain power, and Einstein used only 20 percent of his. Those of us who are devotees of Microsoft Office Suite products (whether we're running a

MAC or not and whether we like it or not) probably realize that we're only utilizing a quarter of what, say, PowerPoint can do. Within the pages that follow, the world of web conferencing is presented in a comprehensive form not available, currently, anywhere else.

A Little Guidance Can't Hurt

When Liz started her own journey into the world of web conferencing, the first thing she did was a global search on Google.com, Yahoo.com, and other search engines to find out what was out there. These searches yielded page after page of links to web conferencing vendor sites and a wealth of technical information about the technology in general and their products in particular. And so the learning project was underway. The first lesson learned was that there is more to web conferencing than one might think.

What do you find when you visit these websites? They are almost as difficult to navigate as a user manual that accompanies a VCR. If you do your own Internet search, you'll find information about the types of web conferencing products, services offered, and the focus of these products and services. Are they best leveraged for sales, marketing, events, or just lately, training and customer support functions?

You'll also be able to download information pertinent to web conferencing, but you won't find much help there with what to do with it if you do download it. Feature lists of the products are big, as are system requirements to run them. Pricing information, however, is a bit harder to find, and while not being as bad as some high-tech shell game, pricing in web conferencing is, well, let's say interesting.

Communications strategies and platforms, and by this we are referring to the hard-core techie information so near and dear to Sue's heart, are also available. Then, consider the vocabularies of these sites. Words like "collaborate," "switching," "proprietary," "browser," "router," and "firewall" are used to sheer exhaustion, but no explanation of their relevance. Marketing information, links to press releases, offers for free demos galore all hit you before you've even left the homepage.

It's almost as if these vendors, without exception, want to attract you with sheer dazzle, and they will explain how the product or service works and how you get your hands on it all in good time. We saw nothing of an explanatory nature on these sites; the reason for the delay may be that you get an explanation when you actually buy or subscribe to a given service. People like us, however, like to understand what we're buying before we slap our credit card on the counter.*

The point is that the vendors assume you already understand the technology. Luckily, after reading this book, you really will understand it.

What's in This Book

This book is written, as you've already surmised, in friendly tones. This is done with purpose because the biggest problem with technology, from the point of view of people like Liz in particular, is that it is really hard to get next to. It's not cuddly, it doesn't seem accessible. It's cold and pushes us away. We didn't want to do that; we specifically want to make you feel as if you are having a conversation about this stuff because indeed, conversing—albeit not entirely by telephone—and broadening one's experience through collaboration is what web conferencing is ultimately all about.

It's important to understand how we all got here, metaphorically speaking, to this place where such ingenious use of bits and bytes is even remotely (ah, another clever pun) possible. So we begin our journey into the land of web conferencing with a look at the evolution of technologies that brought us to this point, starting with audio conferencing—aka, talking on the telephone—to video conferencing and then to web conferencing. And we'll examine what, if anything, are the differences between *communication strategies* and *collaboration strategies*. These two things are not the same, but it's an interesting mindbender as to which one represents the chicken and which the egg. And beyond even that quandary, web conferencing has

---

*We use our credit cards for the miles of course. Just because we are new converts to web conferencing does not mean that we think a virtual safari to Tanzania would cut the mustard. Some travel remains necessary.

evolved from audio and video, but did so without leaving either behind. They are both part and parcel (or could be) of successful use of web conferencing technology.

We'll look at the business justification, the "what's in it for me and my wallet?" aspects of web conferencing. Many reading this book may be in a position to say, "I want this. Go buy it. Damn the budget." But most probably aren't, and so may have to work a bit harder to convince the holders and counters of the beans in Beantown that this is a wicked good investment as they say back in Boston. (Get it? Boston . . . Beantown? Nevermind.)

Go Beyond Why to How

Beyond why you can, and perhaps should, be using web conferencing at work and/or at home, a big part of Chapter Three, which discusses the business case for web conferencing, also discusses how you can best bring this technology to the attention of the people who make the final decision about such utilities and expenditures. This is an area of new technology adoption that the authors have become expert at because we have had to learn to break down one of the areas of resistance—the cost/use barriers to entry—regarding utilizing web conferencing in order to advance our own small businesses.

Web Conferencing in All Its Glory

Chapter Four is particularly important because it's here that the foundation is laid for the next five chapters. "Web conferencing" may be a singular term, but it doesn't manifest itself that way. Our exploration of how and why we might use it in our own small business revealed that it can be used in many different ways and that the most important thing to understand before you choose a technology is your own needs.

Throughout the process of writing this book, we tried to keep a single mantra in mind: "What can web conferencing do for you?" Again, since it turns out it can do a lot, we decided it was best to frame all of the capabilities we encountered as the response to that mantra.

So in Chapter Four, you'll find a snapshot overview of all of the representative products, their features, and functions. You'll also find a description of our sample company, BizMarked, Inc., that we created to use in some of the subsequent five chapters as a user case study. Hopefully this will allow you to see how you might also use one, two, or any combination of the available web conferencing technologies that are, or will be, on the market.

Chapters Five through Nine provide an in-depth look at the technologies we chose to be representative of the functions of web conferencing. See Chapter Four for more details on exactly how all that is broken down.

The Forest for the Trees

Once we've got our completed scorecards for the players, we can look at the field.

So in Chapter Ten, for all you hard-core, hard-ware, hard-wired, hard-facts types out there, we examine all of the technology that is behind all of this technology. Obviously, this is where Sue dominates the keyboard. Even though she's an educated woman, Liz just got that the word "electronics" comes from "electrons."

We'll look at architectures of the products, system requirements, equipment requirements (desktop, mobile, visual/camera, speakers, and microphones), security issues (this is *very* important), and of course, pricing not only for this technology, but for all of the vendors and content providers' products and services. The pricing information is in one of our appendices.

Chapter Eleven looks at the human factors of web conferencing, and this is the other primary barrier to entry that we mentioned earlier when discussing Chapter Three's content about the potential economic and adoption barriers. Indeed, the hardest nuts to crack relative to the successful use of all of these tools have little to do with the tools themselves. They have to do with the people who have to handle the tools. It's true that the younger workers among us are more comfortable at a basic level with all of this than older workers are, but it's not that simple. Even comfort does not guarantee competency or the ability to use a tool to its best advantage. In other words, you can be a young dynamo, fresh out of Harvard Business School with advanced degrees in management and computer science, and you can say that you want to "integrate accounting procedures between the home office and all the satellite offices," but do you have a clue how to do that? Theory in college is a good foundation, but it's not the same as dealing with real systems in the real world.

Or you might be an experienced and well-respected director with five managers working for you who themselves have twenty direct reports each. But all of a sudden, a reorganization demands that now, in addition to your five managers and all their people on site, you will also manage five more managers and all of their direct reports in three additional locations, all in different time zones. This is remote team management in the 21st century, and you've heard about it, maybe even seen it done, but do you know how to do it effectively yourself? These are just two examples of the human factors of web conferencing. There are more. There must be since we have a whole chapter about it.

Chapter Twelve takes us home, literally, to where we discuss the ways that web conferencing technology can be used for fun, to connect with family, to embarrass your kids! Virtual family meetings or reunions are a peace of virtual cake for this technology. Collaborative school projects, hobby groups, book clubs, and fun with photography are some of the uses that can guarantee that between your office and home, you'll never get away from the dang computer. We don't include this use of web conferencing as an afterthought to the business uses. We purposefully include it in this book because we're convinced that as web conferencing becomes more ubiquitous in the workplace—and more familiar to millions of people because of that ubiquity—there will be more interest in using it among family and friends. It's just that home use doesn't require the same amount of functionality or horsepower as business use does, so we want to include a product or two that really has home use firmly in mind. And don't just take our word for it: During the editing process of this book, Microsoft, the maker of NetMeeting, which is the product we chose to highlight for home use (because its' free and comes standard on just about every PC sold in the United States), purchased PlaceWare, a company we chose for its strong story in web conferencing with a focus on collaborative meetings. Can there be much doubt that Microsoft also firmly believes that we stand at the precipice of a web conferencing explosion that will burst out of the office and into our homes? And when's the last time they were wrong about something?

Last, Chapter Thirteen looks ahead at trends. We don't want this book to be obsolete the day it arrives in bookstores, so we had to be on our toes for all of the stuff coming down the road soon (really soon, Liz fears) that we can write about in our second edition. We also invite you to visit the web conferencing section of Sue's company's website at www.switchbacksoftware.com where we will post updates, answer questions, and solicit feedback and progress reports that come as a result of people using this book.

Resources to help you make the decision to use web conferencing effectively in both your professional and personal lives are provided for you in Appendix B. Appendix A looks at the construct and content of effective assessment materials, and Appendix C looks at pricing models.

This is not new technology in the sense that it's just been invented. Web conferencing has been around for about five years now, but it's no where near being commonplace to the point where people are complacent about it. It's commonplace to the point where people are aware and curious. Read on and have your questions answered.

Not Just Talking Heads

Chapter

2

It's not really true that we in society who use technology to any extent woke up collectively about two years ago to find that we were all slaves to it. It just seems that way. It's actually taken longer than that to get its hooks into us, but what with the way things move at the speed of light regarding upgrades and revisions to software or enhancements and improvements to the hardware that software runs on, it's hard to remember the days before we, to use the authors as examples, were the proud owners of three PCs, a laptop, an IPaq, a LAN, two cell phones, a fax machine, a scanner, two PC cameras, three office phones (one wired, one not, and one wireless/headset unit), two printers (one laser, one color), and two satellite dishes. As David Byrne of the Talking Heads once pondered in song, " . . . and you may ask yourself, well, how did I get here?" Good question, David.

You might argue that the authors have all of this stuff because we run businesses out of the house, and you'd be correct. But both of our sets of parents, one set retired, one not, and both sets dedicated to the constant nagging of their children and grandchildren, also have an impressive array of high tech lying about. Among the four of them, our parents have three PCs, a laptop, a portable word processor, two fax machines, four cell phones, two printers (both color), two scanners, one PC camera, and a shredder (don't ask).

Our parents, and probably yours and the rest of your family and just about everyone that you know, have a lot of this equipment, too, because they might not live on the Net, but it sure is a part of their lives. Whether they are sending you emails or doing some online shopping or research or picture swapping, the majority of the developed world is plugged in to an extent they would not have dreamed of in the early 1990s.

The point is, you don't have to be running a business out of your home or otherwise to be both able, and likely, to use technology in ways that ten years ago still seemed as futuristic as the video phone first demonstrated at the 1965 World's Fair in New York. And even though it seems like it all just popped up out of the blue, it didn't.

What Was Bell Thinking?

The telephone is vitally important as the jumping-off point for our look at the evolution of the technology that has culminated not only in our impressive collection of surge protectors, but that brought us to this precipice of web conferencing that very well may be the last technological frontier to fully exploit as regards human communications. Without acknowledging and understanding the telephone, we can't understand how we got to this leading, bleeding edge.

It's interesting that Alexander Graham Bell was not even trying to invent the telephone, or as he might have put it at the end of 19th century, a mechanical way to engender voice communications over distance. He was trying to capitalize and expand upon the telegraph technology available in his day to produce a multiple telegraph; a duplex that could send two messages simultaneously was available by the early 1870s, but Bell, Edison, and a man named Gray were all trying to manufacture one that could send four, six, eight, or more messages.[1]

So, it's an interesting story and we invite and encourage you to check out the full article as noted in the footnote, but we'll cut to the chase. It all really came down to Bell's fiddling about with electricity, vibrations, resonance, and tone. While still in pursuit solely of the multiple telegraph, he started to integrate an area of expertise he had that Gray and Einstein did not: Bell was a teacher of the deaf, and so he was also working on a way to give deaf children a visual representation of sound.[2] It was this work that led him to the realization that vibrations could be translated into electricity and reproduced as sound.

So, lots of transceivers and magnets and electrical currents later, Bell hit upon the fact that what he was trying to create, beyond the multiple telegraph, was a mechanical model of how the human ear works as a receptor of electrical impulses and sound waves that our brains turn into discernable discourse or other recognizable noise. That is the incredible oversimplification of what Alexander Bell did. His efforts culminated in the now famous phrase, "Watson, come here. I need you," which is the quote attributed to Bell as the first words spoken to his assistant, obviously named "Watson," on March 10, 1876, over the instrument we all know as the telephone.

From there, working with the aforementioned Mr. Watson (who actually seemed to do a lot of the work from what we read), Bell designed the actual mechanical instrument; once it was designed, the technology of voice currents carried over distances great and small was a bit of a slam dunk.

The telephone, all these years later, is a remarkable invention that is at the basis of so much of what we take for granted in communication. And it turns out, it's a pretty simple thing, so simple in fact, that what we call an antique phone from the 1920s would, with the proper jack spliced onto its wire, work just fine in your house today.[3]

The Inner Truths of Phones and Phone Networks

There are three parts to any telephone: a switch that connects and disconnects the instrument from the network (the "hook"), a speaker, and a microphone. When first invented and introduced into general use, phones came only in a rotary dial mode, and they only came as those stylish black numbers you see in all the old Jimmy Cagney movies. You had to rent them from the phone company, and you got no choice as to style or color. That would send Martha Stewart over the edge, you think? Although she may have other things on her mind these days.

At this point, we're talking about the period of time after the days of party lines and operators who dialed all the calls for you, that we've conveniently skipped in this story, but the basic technology from those two eras of telephony were similar. That is to say, they both relied on pulses; you could dial a number by tapping the hook (the thing you hang the handset up on, today commonly referred to as the *flash*) the number of times you wanted to dial in pulses, or you could dial a "4" on the rotary unit and as the dial came back, it would emit 4 pulses that you could hear. Liz is old enough to remember this; Sue was born into the world of push-button dialing.

Push-button dialing is, of course, the standard today, and as we'll see in a moment, it's really important, perhaps the most important innovation of the telephone after the invention of the phone itself, for enabling the audio conferencing that, we promise, we're getting to.

It Takes a Certain Touch

We said that an antique phone would work as well in your house as a modern, multilined, speakerphone, caller ID synchronized, answering machine, mute-enabled unit does, and it would. But today's phones, beyond these added conveniences (or annoyances, depending on your outlook), also include a bell (or some other "ringer"), frequency generator, a duplex coil, which blocks the sound of your own voice from getting back to you and driving you insane, and a Touch-Tone keypad.

Let's look at the importance of Touch-Tone. Without it, just about every feature we typically assign to our phones and phone systems would not be possible. You would not be able to have phone extensions at work, or multiple lines in your house that you could switch back and forth, to and from with a simple little toggle. You could not have call waiting, call forwarding, or caller ID. You could not put people on hold, and you could not have audio conferencing, which is about dialing people at multiple locations or extensions simultaneously and allowing them to all share a line.

But just before we get to that, we have to look at one other aspect of telephoning that we all take for granted: the telephone network (see Figure 2.1).

Figure 2.1. A typical telephone network configuration.

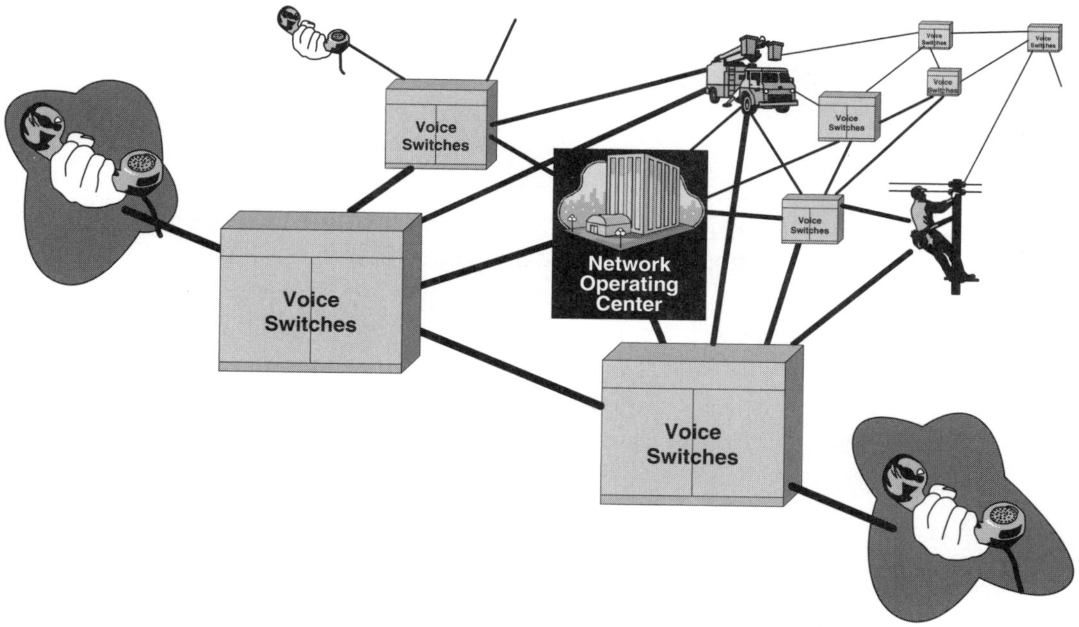

Telephone Networks Most of the Time

The network connects the phones and phone lines that you have in your home or office to the world via a box called an entrance bridge. Copper is the common wire choice for these connections, including those in your building and the telephone cable that runs outside, which is packed with a hundred or more copper pairs. Sooner or later, the cable will end up at the phone company's switch, either directly or by use of a digital concentrator that does pretty much what its name implies. It digitizes your voice (it goes really fast, too) and then combines your voice with others and sends them all down to the phone company via a coax or fiber-optic cable. When all these wires reach the switch at the phone company, they are connected to a line card and you are on line. We believe, although we are not sure, that this is where the phrase "on line" came from. If it didn't, it should have.

Beyond this, depending on how far your voice needs to go, it's carried through a system of switches or perhaps by microwave or satellite or other cool stuff like that. But no matter how far you can call, how clear it is, and how fast it all happens, it's all just about the transmission of electrical impulses and tones over completed circuits. Telephone use is all about completing an electrical circuit, nothing more, nothing less.

When you pick up your phone, you hear a dial tone because the circuit's completion is sensed by the switch and sends the impulse through. When you dial a number, the dialing sounds are actually pairs of tones being sent at different hertz that represent different numbers. When a combination is completed, it takes your instrument out into the network to connect to the instrument that matches the tones you've sent out, and you are connected. That's why operators said, and still say, "happy to connect you." Sorry to disappoint you, but they are not referring to a human connection; they're referring entirely to the physical, electrical one.

The Technology of Audio Conferencing

Besides a telephone or two, audio conferencing requires tones, switches, and bridges. Of these, tones, or what we commonly refer to as touch-tones, are the most important.

Tones are electronic impulses measured in hertz cycles typically in the range of between 400-hertz and 3400-hertz. The sound that you hear when you put your phone to your ear (the dial tone) and the sounds you hear when you dial a number are the result of pairing tones at different cycles to produce different sounds. This ability to differentiate function by tone is what enables the various services a phone provides these days, including the ability to connect more than one person at a time on the same call, which is the essence of audio conferencing.

The different tones connecting various parties to the same call are handled by the switches, which are the mechanisms by which tones that have been cycled to the same number are linked to each other. The bridges are the hardware infrastructures that connect switches to each other all over the planet, and given cellular and satellite communications, above the planet too.

The great thing about audio conferencing when it began to be used a lot was that it let any number of people, a number limited only by the capacity of the network,* talk to one another simultaneously. But the problem with it was, and is, that all you can do is talk. For sure, the emergence of audio conferencing, coming before the LANs (local area networks) and WANs (wide area networks) and pervasive use of email that we are all so used to today, was a big improvement in communication style, if only because when Mr. Big wanted to tell everyone something, he could do it himself without relying on the message getting messed up in its transmission from one person to another. You know that game called "Telephone" where you put, say, ten people in a line and the first one whispers a message to the second that is passed on until it reaches the last person who then repeats what she's been told to the delight of all concerned who see the absurdity of the mangled message? Well, there's a reason they call that game "Telephone."

Audio conferencing helped make sure that everyone involved, at least everyone who was on that conference call, got the message as it was intended, but all of the visual and tactile cues that humans rely

---

*Network in this instance is defined as the system of switches and bridges that your phone capabilities consist of.

on so much to communicate subtext were absent. It's one thing to be able to work a conference call in your pajamas; it's quite another to not be able to see the facial expressions or body language that add so much to communication.

Audio conferencing technology was grasped onto because it was a big improvement over the one-to-one, strictly linear phone conversations that preceded it. Use of guidelines for meetings, learning opportunities, marketing events, sales calls, use of peripherals, and presentation standards were developed for audio conferencing that enabled users to get the most out of the technology.*

But audio conferencing just wasn't good enough.

Say, *Are* Those Pajamas You're Wearing?

The inability to see who you were talking or working with on audio conferences was, to no one's surprise, the biggest driver for companies to try to make video conferencing more stable, more accessible, and more affordable. Two out of three isn't bad. The technologies of video conferencing are more stable and more accessible (if you are a large organization with the proper infrastructure), but none of the vendors have really succeeded in making them what most would call "affordable." Video conferencing remains a wealthy organization's option.

Video conferencing was intended to do two things:

1. Add moving video images to audio to enhance communications.
2. Transmit the video and the audio interactively and two-way.[4]

In order to do these two things, according to John Rhodes in his book, *Videoconferencing for the Real World*, a whole range of tech-

---

*Although beyond the scope of this book, there is at least one excellent set of guidelines for developing content for and utilizing audio conferencing effectively by Ingrid Stammer of Academic Technologies for Learning that can be found at www.atl.ualberta.ca/articles/conf/audio.cfm. Canadian, but they'll work just fine in the States too.

nologies need to come together for the best use of video conferencing. These include digital networks, different communications protocols, computer graphics (titling and captions), digital audio and video compression, ergonomics (we think he's pushing it here, but what the heck, we'll give it to him), interactive multimedia, application-sharing, and acoustical engineering.

The preceding paragraph explains the expense problem. Look at the last item for example, "acoustical engineering." What does this mean? This means that video conferencing must take place in a room where the acoustics will support effective audio communications that are not too low, not too loud, not static-laden or choppy, and so on, and all on a two-way basis. This implies, or flat out says, that the rooms where video conferences take place must be specially designed conference rooms for that purpose. That is not to say that you couldn't use these for regular, face-to-face meetings, too; of course you could. But they must be equipped and built to support video conferencing. That's expensive!

Liz recently participated in a video conference for a big company that has a headquarters in New York and literally dozens of large and small satellite offices elsewhere.

Liz participated in the video conference from this company's offices in Houston with participants conferencing in from Florida, California, Oklahoma, and Nevada. The room she was working from was a well-appointed conference room with the capacity for a very large table or for myriad seating arrangements. It was also equipped with a podium that housed controls for every function in the room—everything from laptop projection to the temperature. From these controls, you could dim the lights, activate any number of microphones, work a digital recorder to record the session, control the TV monitors and the direction of the two wall-mounted cameras, and you could operate the screen in the room for size and backlighting—an impressive setup. The conference was great because this company invested in that technology. So video conferencing is not a bad thing; it's just not an inexpensive thing.

It's also not an uncomplicated thing, in the way that the telephone is an uncomplicated thing. Any organization doing any amount of video conferencing is also maintaining a staff for it. And while video conferencing does indeed afford an effective strategy for two-way communications, it really is effectively limited to two. By that we mean, in a video conference such as the one Liz participated in, everyone in the remote locations knew that Liz was speaking because she was the primary facilitator of the program. Liz, however, only had the name of a contact in New York City, and when he spoke, she could tell because he was the only one whose room was also fully set for video/audio conferencing. If anyone else spoke in New York or elsewhere, Liz could not immediately tell who was speaking or where the question or comment was coming from. So you can have multiple sites participating in video conferencing, but unless every site is fully equipped, it's still a very fancy one-to-many toy with a limited amount of many-to-many communications capabilities.

Which Leaves Us . . .

As we said about audio conferencing, and as we will say about web conferencing, standards of use and applications for video conferencing are rampant and varied. Everything from presentations to large, remote audiences (which is a terrific use of video conferencing), to training, to sales, to marketing has been reengineered to work utilizing this high-tech toy. But as we said before, unless a video conference is going out to places where the technology to receive and respond is as good as the originating point, this is not a collaborative technology. It is a communications strategy to be sure, but not a collaboration strategy.

So now, Watson (as in Sherlock Holmes, and not Alexander Graham Bell), the game is afoot.

It's the Collaboration, Stupid

Communication, as per Webster, is the exchange of thoughts, messages, or information. *Collaboration* is working together, especially in a joint intellectual effort. And there it is, simply put. When we communicate, we talk about something, reason it through, seek to enlighten and to foster understanding. When we collaborate, we *do* something.

Collaboration is kinetic, involving, active, and never passive. You can be *communicated to,* but you can only be *collaborated with.*

The evolution has led us here, to this place where we can use the tools that a century of insight and technical exploration and innovation has dumped on us. For people more like Sue who are fully ready for it and understand it completely, to people like Liz who sort of get it and know that getting ready is an imperative, the crux is not the technology, but what will we all do with it?

When it comes to web conferencing and its role in either bringing together or contributing to the increasing alienation of human beings, depending on your point of view, we have the choice to ignore its potential to enhance our humanity because, after all, we invented the damn stuff, or to embrace it as a method uniquely capable, given all that's come before it, to help us do things we didn't know we could do with each other.

With audio conferencing and video conferencing, we could and can communicate; with web conferencing, we can take all the best parts of the other two and start to really get stuff accomplished. Let's look now at how you can work to get this technology up and running for you.

Notes

1. Michael E. Gorman, "Alexander Graham Bell's Path to the Telephone," *Technology, Culture and Communications,* SEAs, University of Virginia, www.iath.virginia.edu/albell.
2. Ibid.
3. Michael Brain, "How Telephones Work," www.howstuffworks.com/telephone.htm.
4. John Rhodes. *Videoconferencing for the Real World* (Boston: Focal Press, 2001), p. 3.

The Business Case for Web Conferencing

Chapter

3

I f you're like a lot of people, including us, when you come to the precipice of what may be a good idea—in this case, introducing and using web conferencing in your professional and personal lives—you would like to just go ahead and try it. None of this nasty business around actually learning what it is you're getting yourself into, how it all works, and which of the dozens of solutions is right for you. But unfortunately, it doesn't work that way if you want to come out ahead at the end.

And gosh darn it, when it comes to a professional or business use of web conferencing, you can't even jump right into some sort of implementation phase because you're typically spending the company's money and they get so testy about that. Rather, you have to start with investigation where you ask yourself questions such as: Why should we even consider bringing this in-house, and if we agree that we should, how should we best go about it given everything we've already got and the way we conduct our business? Only after these two rather large questions are answered, the why and the how, can you go to the next step, which is to identify the specific product or products that will satisfy your requirements. So answering those questions is exactly what we're going to do before we get into all the specifics of the vendors and their cool toys.

This chapter concerns itself with the myriad elements of why and how. Both consist of a whole lot more than you would have thought, but that's okay; that's why you have us. Right now, we are all about how you sell web conferencing to your own organization.

Lead, Follow, or Get Run Over

Human beings take a while with new stuff: new ideas, new paradigms, new flavors. We fight these changes ferociously sometimes, and one of the first questions that the people holding the purse strings are bound to ask about new technology is, "Is it going to stick around long enough to be worth the time, energy, and money we invest?"

In a September 1999 report from Frost & Sullivan, *U.S. Audio and Document Conferencing Markets,* the annual growth rate for the entire conferencing industry (audio, video, and web), compounded, for the period of 1998–2005 was projected to be 15.2 percent. What they called the "audio and document conferencing services" portion accounted for 81 percent of total market revenues within that growth pattern. As it turns out, web conferencing use to 2002 has surpassed those predictions; interestingly, video conferencing is expected to survive and even prosper in a more limited capacity where it is very effective, such as for those one-to-many explosive announcements.

Web conferencing in and of itself is too new to have generated statistics about the growth of its adoption, but anecdotally, it's destined to be widely adopted faster than any technology that's preceded it. Here's why. It took close to one hundred years for the telephone to become commonplace in every home and office. Video conferencing took forty years to get any serious play, and email, which was available on the desktop by 1980, took twenty years to become the seemingly vital communication tool that it is for millions of people. Based on these trends, industry experts we spoke to believe widespread adoption of web conferencing for all manner of collaborative communications is less than five years away. By 2007 or 2008, we'll all be wondering how (if?) we ever did it all any other way.

What does this portend for the business case? Simple. No one wants to be left behind when the rest of the world starts using the next greatest thing. The Internet itself is a perfect example. Once people started surfing the Net liberally around 1996, it took less than a year for every major organization you can think of to have secured its domain name and put a webpage up. It might not have been pretty, but it was up there. The same will apply to web conferencing. If everyone else is communicating using its many options, no one is going to want to be in the position of not having it at their disposal.

Everything Costs Something

When looking at bringing web conferencing in-house, and especially when trying to justify doing so, the first major factor to come under consideration will be, to no one's great surprise we're sure, cost. One of the major expenditures affected by web conferencing is business travel. There are other considerable cost considerations, but travel is as good a place to start as any.

It is not uncommon for people to assume that if you adopt web conferencing, what you're trying to do is get rid of your travel expenditures totally, as if web conferencing, like video conferencing before it and audio conferencing before both of them, is a substitute for travel. It's not, and as we'll see in our section about overcoming common resistance to web conferencing, trying to position it as such is not a winning gambit for gaining its acceptance. It's better, and frankly more realistic, to position web conferencing as effective augmentation to travel.

In a report called "Meetings in America, A WorldCom Conferencing White Paper," which was prepared by INFOCOM in 1998, the following statistics and assumptions were used to study the cost savings between traveling and remote conferencing:

- Travel savings can be separated into hard (flights, hotels, meals, ground transportation) and soft (saved employee time) savings.

- The average domestic business trip has a hard cost of $1,334 per meeting participant.

- The average business meeting consists of five participants, four of whom have to travel to get to the meeting.

- For the purposes of the report, the average business traveler's annual compensation was set at $80,000/year with another 25 percent of that amount contributed for benefits, yielding an hourly employee cost of about $50.

- The savings in hours between doing a remote conference (four hours for prep and participation) and actually traveling to a place (twenty-one hours invested in flying time, driving time, prep time, the meeting itself, and follow-up tasks) was determined to be, on average, seventeen hours per meeting participant.

So using these statistics and assumptions, the Report concluded that, "at $50/hour, this yields a savings of $850 in soft costs (time saved = 17 × 50) per participant, per converted meeting. By combining the hard cost ($1,334) and soft cost savings, we find that a total of $2,184 can be saved per employee. Applying this savings calculation to all traveling meeting participants reveals that converting the average business travel meeting to a (remote) conference allows an organization to realize a savings of more than $8,000 per meeting."

Keep in mind that these figures are from 1998, and so will be dangerously close to obsolete on two levels at the time you are reading this book. For one, the cost of web conferencing has gone down about 25 percent across the board for all vendors since they've been offering their products and services while the cost of travel has done nothing but rise. So if WorldCom wasn't busy with the SEC or Congress these days, and they were to redo this study to reflect 2002/2003 cost realities, we think it's a good bet that the savings potential for web conferencing would be found to be even higher over travel than it was before the turn of the 21st century.

Productivity Matters

The bottom line is that there is no doubt that web conferencing represents a savings over business travel, and not only in pure dollars. There are other things that are saved as well, not the least of which is time. Now time can be, and frequently is, equated with money, and rightfully so. It's certainly part of the saved money scenarios laid out by the WorldCom report. The seventeen hours we're using as our standard as saved by conferencing rather than traveling to a meeting also results in less wasted time by attendees, including the time they spend arranging a business trip, doing the actual traveling, or waiting in airports due to weather or missed connections. We're also referring to the loss of work they would have accomplished in their primary place of business. Don't imagine that all those business travelers are keeping up with their work on the plane either. A Harris Survey conducted for Delta Airlines reported that only 5 percent of business travelers consider themselves focused on work while they are on an airplane. Instead of working while flying, 81 percent said they read for pleasure, 64 percent relax or fall asleep, and 55 percent watch the in-flight movie or listen to the audio feed.

So what we're saying is that if you can keep your employees at their home base more, you will not lose the time they spend traveling, and you'll also gain work accomplished because you're keeping them in a place where it's relatively certain their exposure to first-run films, the new Springsteen CD, and John Grisham novels is limited.

What else can web conferencing save you and your colleagues? Well, your sanity, for one thing. Although there are some perks associated with business travel that we'll discuss in a moment, anyone who does or has traveled for business to any extent knows that, for the most part, it's a complete and total drag.

Cutting down on business travel cuts down on physical wear and tear and also on stress, and that was never so true as it is post-September 2001. In addition to many people's fears of traveling, security measures have made travel increasingly unreliable and inconvenient.

Quality of Life

In the business world, quality of life might be just some fruity-crunchy-yogurt-granola way of sneakily hammering on productivity, but surely another long-term effect of the way the world changed so dramatically in a single day, and one that probably won't fade away with time, is the way people value their own lives.

During the 2000 International Symposium on Stress, information was provided about stress as relates directly to business travel and also to effects on family life. Seventy-three percent of respondents said that business travel was stressful to them, and more that half of that 73 percent also reported that business travel negatively affected their life, their sleep, their overall well-being, and their general performance both before and after their trip(s). Further, just about 100 percent of the respondents' spouses or partners said that business travel has a negative impact on the stability and happiness of their family life.

Another report, this one from the World Bank, determined that 76 percent of business travelers suffer from more health problems when they travel. The World Bank went on to report that frequent business travelers are three times more likely to use their corporate health programs for mental health assistance.

This is not to say that most people, or even a small percentage of business travelers, don't enjoy the journeys at all. There are some perks associated with business travel, like the ability to break your routine and cut loose away from the office; or to tack on a day or two in some destination you've always wanted to visit and do it on the company's dime; or perhaps see friends and family who happen to be where you need to go; or rack up those frequent traveler miles and points so you can take the family away someplace really cool soon. However the clear implication of the data provided here is that most business travelers don't really like it and would limit how much travel they have to do for work. Web conferencing can help establish and maintain those limits.

Power to the People, Right On

According to Andrew Davis in his paper on Conferencing and Collaboration, remote conferencing can be thought of as operating in three distinct ways: as conferencing, which is real-time, two-way communications; as casting, which is real-time, one-way broadcasts; and as caching, which is non–real-time communications. And according to Mr. Davis, any of these three conferencing categories may contain any mix of audio, video, and data.[1]

Of the three conferencing technologies available—audio, video, and web—only web conferencing offers access to all available media in all three of Davis' categories. Further as a desktop centric technology, web conferencing represents (or will as soon as people are more used to it) the same sort of instant access to others that the telephone does. In other words, if your telephone rings and you're there to answer it, then the connection between you and the other party or parties is made. If you're not there, then probably a message is taken one way or another.

If someone wants to initiate a web conference with you, he'll call or email or instant message you to initiate the conference. If you're there, you're there; if not, your computer will be able to log the attempt so you'll know that someone was trying to reach you. No need really to prearrange the meeting unless that is the standard for whatever you are working on, and certainly no need to arrange to be in a certain room with certain equipment at a certain time. The ability of individual workers to take advantage of the enormous collaboration features inherent in all web conferencing products will be in the near future, if it's not already, the purview of any and all organizations with even a rudimentary networking infrastructure.

So the number one benefit of web conferencing is that it is not just for the fat cats with the fancy conference rooms; it's a little person's technology. Power to the people indeed. A summary of other benefits of web conferencing follows:

- Savings in both hard costs and soft costs; web conferencing is a cheaper way of accomplishing certain elements of the business.
- Savings in individual and organizational time; this savings contributes directly to productivity.

- Improved quality of life and overall health, physical and mental, of your employees.

- Simplified access to others inside and outside of the organization with almost no advance notice, just as with a phone call.

- More effective teamwork among people working on the same project but from different locations is enhanced by the full-scale media sharing capabilities of web conferencing.

- Lower training costs lend themselves very well to this technology (as we'll see in Chapter Seven, which deals with web conferencing content), and that can mean greater access by more personnel at a lesser cost for these programs.

- Staff remain in their primary office location, where they are typically more productive.

- More robust than both video conferencing, which only lets you see the other parties you're working with but not share pertinent data or documents or exhibits; and certainly more robust than audio conferencing, which allows strictly voice communications. The additions of tactile and visual capabilities of web conferencing technologies we'll examine over either of the other two allow for increased impact of the meeting, increased participation by everyone connected, and therefore, faster results.

Not So Fast . . .

Before you get the impression that we think web conferencing is the absolute answer to every ill that can befall an organization, we should make it clear that this is not the case. We alluded before to the fact that web conferencing should *not* be positioned as a substitute for travel, and the reason for that is because it doesn't work well for everything that businesses accomplish using travel. These conferencing technologies, as you'll see in Chapters Five through Nine, can do some really amazing things both in general terms and for specific types of tasks, but frankly what none of them can do at all is replace a handshake. And as most people in business know, a handshake and all it implies can be the most important part of some business interactions.

Becky Replogle-Wilkes, Director of Collaborative Applications Marketing for Sprint Corporation put it like this, "Do I really need to meet this person face-to-face to achieve my goal? Sometimes the answer is yes, as when it's time to meet a sales prospect for the first time, to conduct a final interview with a job candidate, or to hold an all-day session in one time zone."[2]

So, web conferencing should be brought in-house for meetings; project management across teams, departments, or the enterprise; recruiting efforts, sales calls, PR, and marketing announcements; internal HR policy distribution and some training. However, keep in mind that there are some things you will still have face-to-face, even if it means boarding a plane or taking a drive.

Oh No, We Couldn't Possibly

Even after working through the cost, productivity, and wear-and-tear on people issues, you will still face resistance. These resistance factors are:

1. Technophobia
2. Lack of knowledge
3. Employees who are not comfortable with change
4. Leaders who are not sure where to begin and how to make the right choices
5. Top executives (or purse-string holders) who are not computer or Internet users
6. Hesitation about being seen on video camera
7. System security

Of these seven resistance factors, technophobia is probably the most important and perhaps is as far as the discussion need go. The good news is that a phobia, by definition, is illogical (look it up). That means that technophobia can be overcome by applying logic to it.

Let's examine some of these resistance factors in more depth. To start, consider how many of the resistance factors can be directly attributed to ignorance. We don't mean ignorance in any value-judgment sort of way. We mean ignorance of the facts of the matter. We all start out ignorant every time we turn down a new road, so there's nothing to be embarassed about. A good way to overcome resistance to change when change is perceived to be intrinsically bad is to go back and review all the ways that the organization has absorbed changes in the past. All organizations change aspects of their operations constantly; it's just that some changes are more subtle than others.

A lot of what you will read about web conferencing in the rest of this book deals with not only the technologies and tools, but is about how use of these technologies can positively influence the way people do and think about things. This is powerful stuff and the associated growing pains can be hard, but can be made easier if you remind people that they've done it before, and for better, not for worse.

One last point along these lines: The way that you choose to implement your web conferencing strategy will go a long way toward its success or failure. Since actual implementation is where the rubber meets the road for real people using web conferencing, you'll find more discussion about implementation strategies in Chapter Eleven.

Take It to Your Leaders

In so far as resistance from any aspect of your leadership is concerned, it's very important to understand where the decision makers are on an issue so you can approach them on whatever level they're ready for. The good news is once you know where your executives are in the learning curve about web conferencing, you can introduce them to the information they need to make informed choices by bringing them up to speed from that place. This will enable them to learn without feeling insecure about their lack of previous knowledge and that's a good thing, because you don't want to make your leadership feel insecure. Leaders who feel insecure are famous throughout history for saying things like "off with their heads!" or making decisions like Waterloo.

As for resistance that has at its heart an unfamiliarity with technology or a low comfort level about it, the solution is relatively simple: convince non-users of technology to give it a whirl by gently showing them what it is capable of. If that means that before showing an executive that she can whiteboard and download brainstorming sessions with her peers with web conferencing you have to first show her how to forward an email message while deleting content from it that she might not want forwarded, or even how to create folders for organization of her email, then so be it. That's what you should do.

Image Is Everything

Audio conferencing might be severely limited in its ability to take advantage of the best ways that people grasp and retain information, which are visually and kinetically, but it's awfully good at not letting other participants see your bad hair day. Personal image is important to most people, so be sensitive to people's resistance about whether or not they want other people to be able to see them all of the time. Perhaps it's as easy as explaining to them that all PC cameras have covers and that the choice of whether to see and be seen will be mostly up to them. But whatever you do, don't forget that this might be a big part of a person's problem with adopting the technology.

A Feeling of Security

As for system security, this is a vital consideration when implementing web conferencing, and for that reason, it's covered in detail in Chapter Nine. What we would like to say here is that web conferencing is, these days, browser based. What that means is that if you already operate in an environment that includes local area and/or wide area networking, and that also includes internal and external access to your organization's intranet and to the Internet, then you already have a system of security and firewalls in place that will be sufficient, in conjunction with what the vendors provide for security, to provide security for your data, transmissions, meetings, and seminars.

To Sum Up

Again, if you position web conferencing as the be all and end all, you will invite even more resistance from people who don't want to see it implemented. They will find fault with your argument—for example, that travel is no longer ever necessary (and they'll be right) and then they'll have ammunition to attack other parts of your justifications. So as discussed earlier, be realistic in your positioning the way that web conferencing can, and should be used to augment travel, not replace it.

In short, the key to overcoming all resistance is to understand precisely where the resistance is coming from and address it at that place, not where you wish it was or think it should be, but where it is.

There is a great deal of evidence to suggest that remote conferencing technologies are not only viable and smart solutions for any organization that wishes to cut costs without sacrificing operational effectiveness, but that their broad use by organizations of all kinds the world over is inevitable. First adapters are getting ahead of this growing snowball by becoming aware of—and investigating—the ways that web conferencing is superior in many respects to audio or video conferencing. Right now perhaps it can be argued that web conferencing is still dependent on 20th century telephony or that it is too unsophisticated to effectively carry video, but as you'll see in the coming chapters, it doesn't do either one all that badly and it will only improve in both areas.

Resistance to adopting web conferencing mirrors in many ways the resistance to change that many pacesetters are familiar with; the good news is that for that reason, there's a lot of methodology out there to help overcome the resistance.

Notes

1. Andrew W. Davis, *Conferencing and Collaboration: Applications in Transition* (Brookline, MA: Wainhouse Research, 2002) www.wainhouse.com.
2. Carolyn Hirschman, "Workforce: Alternatives to Business Trips Can Pay Off," Wainhouse Research (1995–2001), www.wainhouse.com.

What It Can All Do for You: An Overview

Chapter

4

The reason it occurred to Liz that there was more to this web conferencing thing than meets the eye on first glance is because there is. There's not only more than one vendor skinning this cat, there's a ton of ways they're skinning it. It's safe to say that all of the vendors included here have their own philosophies about what works best when using this technology, but it goes beyond that too. It goes to where their philosophies led them to develop their strengths.

The various strengths of the range of web conferencing products available on the market will be the most important factor in your decision to bring web conferencing in-house. You'll have to map those strengths to your needs for web conferencing in order to pick the product, or products, to best meet those needs. To do that, you must understand where all the available products are coming from.

Chapters Five through Nine offer very detailed descriptions and explanations of products that are representative of the capabilities of web conferencing. But before diving into them all, it behooves us to lay a foundation of knowledge about how the products are characterized and what some of the less-commonly known terminology means that flows so freely when web conferencing is the topic of conversation. This way, when you start reading about the products in detail, you'll understand what you are reading. At least, that's the plan.

How the Products Are Categorized

To write this book, the first question we needed to answer for ourselves was, do we look at these products based on our needs or based on their functions? We chose their functions because our needs, as small business owners, are not necessarily representative of the needs of any other small business, or certainly of any medium to large to giant business. Categorizing by function seemed the best way to make sure that the categories mean something to anyone at any organization of any size who might be considering this technology.

Functional Breakdown/Vendors Who Deliver This Function

1. General Business Communications: These are products that offer multifaceted, but integrated, capabilities to host meetings, do broadcasts, hold training sessions, and perform customer service and support tasks.

2. Project Management: These are products that let people see how one thing leads to another, and who is doing what, on a project large or small. For example, let's say that BizMarked wanted to completely revamp the way they do the tracking of their service contracts. Right now, they are tracking service contracts for their clients by date, but this is becoming impractical because so many of their clients are running myriad technologies that they are adding to or changing all the time. BizMarked has decided to break down everything that they support for a given client by the product instead of by the contract start date. And because their clients are adding/changing what they are running all the time, BizMarked must be able to set up each client with a list of everything they are running. This requires coordination of databases at BizMarked's headquarters in Denver and in all nine of their satellite offices. There is a project manager in all ten offices and each of them has a staff of two to three people working on the project. In order to keep track of everything, BizMarked elects to use a web conferencing software specifically designed with project

management in mind. This is the sort of product we examine in Chapter Six.

3. Voice and Voice Over IP Centric: Not every vendor has a fully integrated voice system to offer along with their web conferencing capabilities, and even though most companies have a reliable voice network they can use to augment their web conferencing efforts, there's a lot to be said for integration. Voice over IP, in particular, refers to using the same Internet connection for voice as for data, video, and so on during a web conference. It's not perfect yet . . . but they're getting there.

4. Content Delivery Specialists: Having the technology is one thing, knowing what to do with it is definitely another. There are three ways to look at web conferencing content: vendors who have tools to help you design your own; vendors who have pre-packaged content you can buy, edit, and distribute asynchronously (not in real time); and vendors who have content that is provided by live facilitators synchronously (in real time).

5. Mostly Meetings/Small Business Focus: These are products that are the result of vendors having really spent a wad on their ability to provide for collaborative, interactive meetings and who also focus on economy of scale.

Terminology

In order to understand the capabilities of web conferencing, it's very important that you understand all the words we'll use to describe its features and functions and how those add value for you. Chapters Five through Nine contain a lot of technology-centric language, most of which we are confident you'll be fully familiar with. But there may be new terms too, so we've made a list and offered basic definitions.

Agent—Some person or object that can access your system remotely during a web conference.

Annotating—The ability to mark up, edit, comment upon, or explain something on a document, picture, slide, schematic, and so on that is being collaborated upon during a web conference.

Application sharing—The ability for any application, regardless of protocol or type, to be transmitted to all parties on a web conference. In some cases, applications can be freely shared whether all web conference participants are running the applicable software or not.

ASP: Active Server Pages—A tool for creating content on web-pages used by software developers.

Asynchronous—Communication that doesn't have to take place in real time. In the context of web conferencing, asynchronous communication means that people can collaborate on materials at their convenience.

Bchannel—The transmission types on an ISDN network are called channels. Bchannels are "Bearer" channels that are used for voice or up to 64Kbps of data.

Bandwidth—The capacity of a wire, cable, signal, or any other method of data transmission.

Blended Content—Refers to content on web conferences that is both live and pre-recorded or pre-packaged.

Branding/Branded Participant—The ability to put your own logo on a web conferencing screen, regardless of which web conferencing vendors' product(s) you are using. A Branded Participant has "branded" the collaborative screens with its logo or other identifying mark.

Breakouts—The ability for people to break out into smaller groups, independent of other small groups, and work on materials or assignments adjunct to the main web conference.

Broadcast/Narrowcast—A broadcast is a general announcement made to a large number of people in many different locations. A narrowcast is a new term, coined in relation to web conferencing, that denotes a large, but more specific group of people, also in different locations, to whom you want to make a general announcement.

Browser—The tool that allows people to go from Internet site to Internet site. Internet Explorer and NetScape are examples of browsers.

B2B—Business to business communications.

Buffer—When data is sent from one place to another, it is frequently sent in batches. The buffer is a "space" where all of the contents of a batch can be put before it is transmitted to the parties on a web conference. Buffers control the speed and resolution at which content is transmitted.

Call control—Managing the way that information is requested from, provided by, servers on a network. A request for information is a "call."

Chat—The ability of two or more people to have a conversation as part of, or adjunct to, web conferencing.

CODEC—A software program used by developers to create digital content on the Internet.

CSDN: Circuit Switched Digital Network—A network that has a dedicated circuit for the duration of a transmission. The kinds of connections that are made with our standard telephone are CSDN connections.

CSP: Conference Service Provider

Custom Tags—A method of coding in Java that is used extensively for webpage development.

Dchannel—The transmission types on an ISDN network are called channels. Dchannel is used for call-control signaling or up to 16Kbps of packet data.

Datagrams—Packets of data sent over a network.

Data sharing—The ability of all members of a web conference (who are given authority by the host or moderator) to see and manipulate files, applications, databases, video, and so on that may be part of the content of the web conference.

Distributed Teams—Workgroups that are physically located in different parts of the world.

Emoticons—Symbols that can be communicated during a web conference to let the moderator or all other participants know how you are feeling about what is going on. These may be symbols that denote "perplexed," "saddened," or "happy," and so on.

Firewall—A software mechanism that provides protection from unauthorized access to an organization's (or individual's) computer, network, data, and so on.

Flash—A generally available protocol for sending both sound and image files over the Internet.

HTML: HyperText Markup Language—Language used to define, or write, webpages consisting of tags.

Hyperlinks—URL links that are displayed on a webpage that you can click on and be taken to the new URL.

Interface—How information, data, objects, or any content of a software program or process is presented to the user; in other words, the format of how people see information on their computers.

ISDN: Integrated Services Digital Network—A network in which the same digital transmission paths are used to establish connections for different services. It can handle voice, data, email, fax, sound, still and moving images unlike other network protocols that can't handle all these kinds of media.

Internet Authority: InterNIC—The organization charged with assigning domain names and URL extensions (like .com or .net or .org) to Internet users. Also a clearinghouse for information related to the worldwide use of the Internet.

IP Address: Internet Protocol Address—Every time (session) a person (or more correctly, a computer) accesses the Internet, the machine is assigned an address on the Internet. Among other things, your session IP address allows other users to find you on the Net.

Java Applet—Java program that can be downloaded and run in a browser.

Load Balancing—The ability of a group of servers in a network, regardless of how many or where they are all located, to monitor how much work one is doing as opposed to the others so as to balance the workload between them. Load balancing results in better, faster, and more reliable network communications.

Nesting/Nested Folders—When data, files, applications, media, or any other content transmitted during a web conference is organized into folders and then those folders are placed one inside another.

Network Node—Any address on a network, but usually a physical device such as a printer or a PC.

Object—In this context, a database, application, still picture, audio clip, video clip, or other media that can be transmitted and shared during a web conference.

On-the-Fly Annotation—Annotation of web conferencing content that takes place as it's being viewed by any participant in the conference who has been given annotative authority by the web conference host or moderator.

Packet Driven—The transmission of data over the Internet typically occurs in groups of data that are called packets.

PBX: Private Branch Exchange—The typical type of phone network found in companies to manage all phone traffic internally and externally.

PDF (Acrobat) Files—Common format used for storing Acrobat files. A free reader is available, which is why so many people use this format for sharing read-only (cannot be edited) information.

Performance Reviews—The ability for a presenter in a broadcast web conference (that is to say one that is going out to a large group of people) to get instant feedback from participants as to how he's doing.

Plug-ins—Additional functionality provided by a third party that can be used by a device such as an Internet browser to run a program that might reside on a website.

Polling—The ability to see how everyone on a web conference is reacting to the information being disseminated. In most web conferencing packages, polling can be done on-the-fly or poll questions can be prepared in advance and then sent out to participants at the appropriate time.

Portal—A way to enter a particular part or site on the Internet.

Private Leased Lines—Telephone or other data lines that are leased by a company or group of companies to handle only their transmissions.

Protocol—An agreed upon set of conventions used between communicating functional units that may be hardware or software.

PSTN: Public Switched Telephone Network—The analog circuit switching system that was (is) the basis for all common telephone networks. Although PSTN is more often than not digital these days, not all telephone users have digital connections.

Reservation-less System—A system for setting up audio conferences that doesn't require that a reservation on the provider's system be made. A monthly fee may be paid that permits 24/7 access by authorized users.

Resolution—The clarity with which web conferencing content is sent and received.

Q&As—Question and answer sessions that can be done on-the-fly or set up in advance during most kinds of web conferences. Q&As differ from polls in that a poll is usually a survey of the whole group on a particular matter while a Q&A typically occurs one user to the moderator at a time.

Scalability—The ability to grow a network or web conference; the degree to which a web conference can be expanded to include the desired number of people even if that number is in the thousands.

Single Interface—When all of the screens of a particular vendor's web conferencing options look exactly alike in terms of format and layout. In other words, some vendors choose to make their training conference center look and act different from their meeting conference center because there are different capabilities in each. Some vendors choose to make all of their interfaces look alike despite differences in functionality.

Still Shots—A still photographic image of an object or a person that is transmitted during a web conference.

Streaming (Audio & Video)—The way that data, images, and sound are transferred over the Internet. Usually parts of the data, called packets, are sent in groups and received in groups. The sending/receiving of these packets is called streaming. Depending on the size of the buffer, streamed audio or video may appear seamless or may appear in slightly separate chunks.

Synchronous—Communication that takes place in real time between people, geographically dispersed as they may be, who are all on a web conference at the same time.

Telephony—The transmission of sound between distant points, especially by electronic or electrical means.

Templates—Pre-formatted forms and interfaces for designing or transmitting information during a web conference.

Threaded Chat—When a chat during a web conference is followed on the screen from the beginning until its end so that everyone who is involved in the chat or who has visibility to it can see the thread of the conversation.

URL: Universal Resource Locator—Used to define a unique resource on the Internet, such as a website.

Verticals—The way of grouping companies or organizations into business categories. For instance, the Financial Services Vertical might include banks, brokerage houses, financial services organizations, and insurance companies. The Technology Vertical might include hardware manufacturers, software developers, peripherals producers, and technical support companies.

VOIP: Voice Over IP—Transmitting voice over the same Internet session as data, video, or other web conferencing content. Typically involves the use of a microphone connected to a PC as opposed to using telephone equipment.

VPN: Virtual Private Network

Whiteboard—The space on most web conferencing products where all applications being shared on the web conference, annotation, or brainstorming takes place.

Wizard—A part of a software program that is like a guide or a help mechanism to show you how to do something.

Looking at the Big Picture

As you read the next five chapters about the various categories of web conferencing and the products we've chosen to represent each, you'll undoubtedly notice that a lot of the features and benefits of the products look and sound alike. For the most part, we did find that to be true, but we also found that some products key on some functions better than others, which is why we put them in chapters that discuss those specific strengths. And we also found that some products do unusual or unique things within their frameworks, and where that occurred to us, we point it out to you.

In terms of what you might expect to get in the way of features/function benefits from a web conferencing vendor you become intrigued about as a result of reading this book, take a look at the matrix from Interwise (see Figure 4.1).

It would be impossible for us to produce such a spreadsheet on a manageable piece of paper that would lay out all of our selected vendors' products like this, but a quick perusal of this one will give you an idea about how most, if not all, web conferencing vendors lay out their products. It's sort of like a site map on a website because it tells you what all of the main areas are and how everything else is nested (See? We already used one of our new vocabulary words.) into those main areas.

A Quick Dissection

The first thing the spreadsheet tells you are the features and functions of the Interwise product. They call their features "modes"; other vendors use "rooms" or "centers" to describe the various web conferencing capabilities they provide.

Figure 4.1. Interwise ECP features by mode.

Features and Functions					
Interwise mode	iMentoring	iMeeting*	iClass	iSeminar	iCast
Size of group	One-on-one	Up to 25	Up to 100	Hundreds	Thousands
Moderator					
Content creation					
Templates for agenda	X	X	X	X	X
Templates for content presentation	X	X	X	X	X
Templates for quizzes, evaluations	X	N/A	X	X	X
PowerPoint	X	X	X	X	X
Word	X	X	X	X	X
Excel	X	X	X	X	X
Adobe Acrobat (pdf)	X	X	X	X	X
Standard audio file formats	X	X	X	X	X
Standard video file formats	X	X	X	X	X
Flash	X	X	X	X	X
Java	X	X	X	X	X
DHTML	X	X	X	X	X
Communication					
Two-way video	X	Multipoint up	X	one-way	one-way
Text chat private to participant	X	X	X	X	X
Text chat public to all participants	X		X	X	X
Control microphone use	X	Unique speak	X	X	X
Control participant hand raising					
Testing and Interactions					
Yes/No polls	X	N/A	X	X	N/A
Free-form testing	X	N/A	X	X	N/A
Multiple choice	X	N/A	X	X	N/A
Ask for OK response	X	N/A	X	X	N/A
Create questions on-the-fly	X	N/A	X	X	N/A
Self-exercise creation for learners	X	N/A	X	X	N/A
Over-the-shoulder viewing	X	N/A	X	X	N/A
Presentation Delivery					
Whiteboard	X	X	X	X	X
Mark-up tools	X	X	X	X	X
File-creation and delivery before event	X	X	X	X	X
File delivery during event	X	X	X	X	
Notification that files have loaded	X	X	X	X	X
Application sharing	X	X	X	X	X
Record event for later viewing	X	X	X	X	X
Create breakout sessions	X	N/A	X	N/A	N/A

(continues)

Figure 4.1 *(Continued.)*

Co-moderators					
Instruct session participants	X	N/A	X	X	X
Answer notes	X	N/A	X	X	X
Assist participants during live event	X	N/A	X	X	X
Talk privately with participants	X	N/A	X	X	X
Participant					
Communication					
Raise hand	X	X	X	X	X
Two-way video	X	X	X	X	X
Mark-up tools	X	X	X	X	X
Text chat private to moderator	X	N/A	X	X	X
Text chat private to other participants	X	X	X	X	
Audio response	X	X	X	X	X
Can leave event temporarily	X	X	X	X	X
Event Materials					
Automatic recording of meeting	X	X	X	X	X
File delivery before event	X	X	X	X	
File delivery during event	X	X	X	X	
Viewing					
Over the shoulder	X		X	X	X
Pre-recorded events	X	X	X	X	X
Testing and Interactions					
Yes/No polls	X	N/A	X	X	N/A
Free-form testing	X	N/A	X	X	N/A
Multiple choice	X	N/A	X	X	N/A
OK response	X	N/A	X	X	N/A
Self-exercise mode	X	N/A	X	X	N/A
Participate in breakout session	X	N/A	X		
Administrator					
Online registration	X	X	X	X	X
Import participant data	X	X	X	X	X
Assign moderators	X	N/A	X	X	X
Automatic email reminders to participants	X	X	X	X	X
Records registration and attendance	X	X	X	X	X
Records event evaluations	X	X	X	X	X
Custom reports	X	X	X	X	X
Exports reports	X	X	X	X	X

N/A = Not applicable

*In iMeeting, there is no moderator; all participants use Participant interface with an automatically queued speaking order.

Next, we see how many people are intended to or can participate in the Interwise web conferencing options.

Then Interwise breaks down the functions of each web conference by what each type of participant can do. What Interwise calls a "moderator" may be called a "panelist," "instructor," or "host" by another vendor; the idea is the same though—this is the person running the web conference and these are the capabilities that she has while running it. Her capabilities are broken down into communication capabilities, presentation capabilities, and sharing some of her duties with designated co-moderators (to use the Interwise lingo).

Similarly participants, who might also be referred to as "students," "members," or "observers" in other products, have capabilities during a web conference. Finally, there is typically an administrator, in some products referred to as a "coordinator," who takes care of the logistics involved in making a web conference run smoothly.

And Just Remember This

There's something else to keep in the back of your mind at all times when you're learning about—and eventually using—these tools: *Web conferencing is about interacting with others, using software, in such a way as to mimic being in the room with them.* Don't forget that, and you'll never stray too far from comprehension as you read.

How It All Can Come Together for You

Now we're ready to explore web conferencing products in depth. Some of the vendors we worked with provided us with some really good actual case studies of others using their products, but not all of them did and not all the case studies cover all of that vendor's capabilities.

So in order to make the information easier for you to relate to, we're going to use a company we've called BizMarked, Inc. as an occasional case study. Where we think that a real-world example is useful to better make a point or a connection to your possible needs, we'll tell you something about BizMarked, Inc. and how the product served it. For now all you need to know is that BizMarked is a 500-person technical support company that provides a range of support services to its clients who themselves are using literally hundreds of different kinds of hardware and software to run their businesses. BizMarked is headquartered in Denver, Colorado, with satellite offices in New York, Boston, Chicago, Dallas, Atlanta, Memphis, Phoenix, Seattle, and San Francisco. It has a reciprocal partnership arrangement with similar organizations in Europe and Asia to provide support services to mutual and differentiated clients. Its employees are, by and large, hardware and software engineers with a typical mix of marketing, finance, and administrative personnel. Its annual revenues are about $40 million and it's been around since 1994.

No, you can't buy stock. Now, let's get started.

Web Conferencing Basics

5

We begin our look at specific products for web conferencing with the products we classified as being good for general business communications. As noted in Chapter Four, these products offer multifaceted, but integrated, capabilities to host meetings, do broadcasts, hold training sessions, and perform customer service and support tasks. We've chosen the web conferencing schemes from WebEx and Interwise to represent the functions and capabilities of these types of collaborative products.

The Wide World of WebEx

We look at WebEx as sort of the grand-daddy of them all. This is not because they were the first player (they weren't) or that they are the biggest (we don't think they are and besides, size is not relevant in cyberspace). Rather we think of them this way because they tell a compelling story about the way they constructed their products, and it's a story that has relevance to everything that follows, whether it be their own products or another vendor's.

WebEx is all about enhancing communications capabilities. From our conversations with WebEx folks, we can attest to the fact that improving human communications and collaboration through software is all they care about. They're fixated on this and they went a long way beyond what was going on technologically at the time they hit the playing field to support their fixation. Although this is not the hard-core technology chapter where we'll explain all the bits and bytes in some detail, if you're going to appreciate the layers and features of this and other web conferencing products, the foundation we provide here will help a lot.

The WebEx Way

The first thing is that WebEx believes that its resolution quality—in voice, video, documentation, web, or on the fly annotation transmission—must be flawless. Their thinking is that part of the reason why telephones are so popular is that no one who uses them typically has to worry about them. We don't have to worry about how they get power, we just plug them into the wall. We don't have to worry about using different instruments to accomplish the same thing in any room of our house or office or now, in the world of cellular and digital technology, anywhere in the world. And we don't have to worry about whether the phone will work if we call a friend in France and she's speaking French while we're speaking English. The telephone doesn't care what language you are speaking or what kind of instrument you are using either. WebEx wanted WebEx to have that same *hakuna matata* sort of interface for all its customers, too (that's Swahili for "no worries"). To accomplish this, WebEx quickly decided that they couldn't depend solely on public networks, either phone networks or Internet backbones. So they just went out and built their own network topography. This resulted in two things that are very important for the effective use of web conferencing: first, that it be reliable and secure, and second, that it permit seamless integration and presentation of anything people could think to transmit over the Internet. In other words, it needed to not matter if complicated product schematics are being viewed at the same time as PowerPoint presentations while participants are also surfing the Web via some search engine and reviewing a Word document too. With a dedicated network, WebEx is able to deliver this kind of reliable, stable, secure, and multifaceted web conferencing platform that is not dependent on other technology.

The WebEx model for seamless integration, access, and transport of everything you could possibly think to throw into a meeting or class is called the WebEx Multimedia Switching Platform, which works in conjunction with the WebEx Interactive Network (WIN). WIN is a fully redundant network; this means it has its own backup plans and fail-safes built in. It is a private, global network specifically designed to deliver real-time communications over the web. It consists of hundreds of servers in ten locations (2002) across the United States, Europe, and Asia.

To sum up, WebEx looked at the state of the digital communications world and decided that if you want it done right, you need to do it yourself. They went ahead and built a better mousetrap that they call their MediaTone Network for live multimedia communications. It is MediaTone, running on the WebEx switches and network, that allows complex and varied media types to be shared at the same time (see Figure 5.1). What WebEx created, therefore, is not unlike what AT&T, the original Ma Bell, had to go out and do when they wanted to put a phone in everyone's hands. They had to create a telephone network where none previously existed.

Figure 5.1. Shows the MediaTone infrastructure. Notice that the WebEx switch boxes mirror the voice switches found in standard telephone network designs.

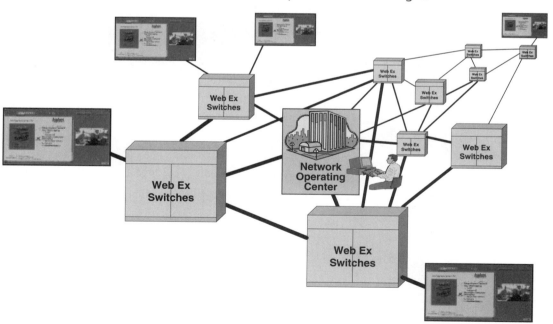

What's important to grasp about this infrastructure at this point is that beyond having its eye on the reliability prize, WebEx at its inception was also focused on simplicity. All the user needs is a computer, access to the Net, a browser, and a phone, or a microphone and speakers. These are things that the user already has and, more important, knows how to use. Any downloading of software or firewall products or plug-ins needed to run WebEx are provided and performed for users the first time they log on to a session, a meeting, a class, or whatever. The technology takes care of it; it's a passive, nonanxiety-causing exercise for the user that can happen at any one of several junctures. Two examples are provided next.

Figure 5.2 shows a setup option screen in WebEx. First-time users click on Setup to set up an account on the system. It asks for profile info, preferences, and it then downloads the security and plug-ins needed to run the programs.

Figure 5.2. Initial WebEx meeting setup screen as displayed on Work Worlds' on-line seminar website.

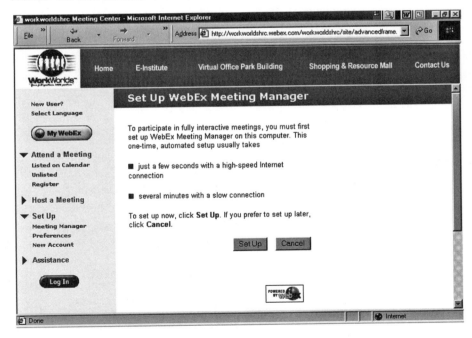

Figure 5.3 shows a "joinameeting" screen. If it were a user's first time joining a meeting, the same setup cues would be offered first because the client has to be established for each user on your system. Note that this setup would also occur if the first WebEx function you joined was not a meeting, but rather was a class or a customer service session and that once established, setup doesn't have to be performed again, although entries can be edited. As with all of the other web conferencing products we'll examine, your organization can customize the look and feel of your WebEx pages to match your organization's (or household's for that matter) standards for network, intranet, or Internet interfaces. However, if your household has standards for network or Internet interfaces, then you need to get out more.

Last thing, WebEx doesn't care if you are a PC user or a Macintosh maven or if you have Solaris or Linux or Unix boxes singly or in combination all over your network, all over the world. It'll work with all of them.

Figure 5.3. The options presented to you in a typical join-a-meeting scenario.

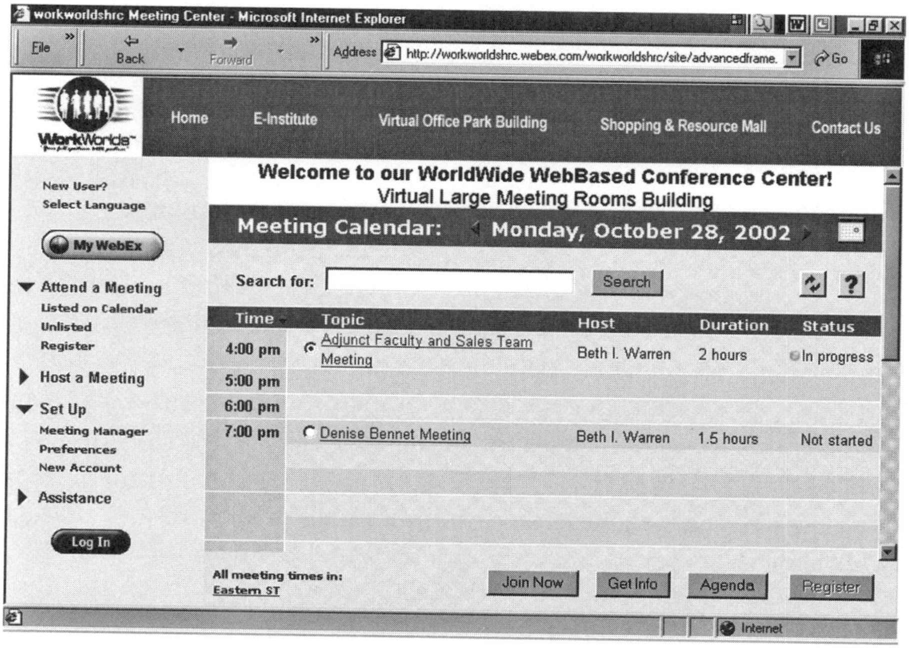

Primary Applications of Web Conferencing

The uses for general business web conferencing fall into five categories:

1. Online Meetings: The core function of web conferencing is to provide online meetings that support digital media, data, video, voice, and telephony.

2. Customer Service Support: Customer service organizations can use web conferencing as an extension of their own customer care websites. WebEx's Support Center enhances an organization's own sites with the ability of service personnel to provide hands-on support to remote users through a standard web browser. In other words, they can both see inside and run your machine(s). For example, let's say a client of BizMarked called their support because his network keeps crashing whenever a specific accounting software program tries to back itself up. Rather than just having to describe the problem so that the BizMarked support rep could try to replicate and solve it, the BizMarked support team rep could actually access the client's server with a support web conferencing product, run the troublesome program himself, see what happens when the machine crashes, and, hopefully, fix it right then and there.

3. Large Meeting Capability: You can use this capability when you want to show people a lot of stuff all at the same time. The functions of this sort of web conferencing are differentiated from regular meeting web conferencing by the ways in which communication back and forth is more limited. Onstage, WebEx's large meeting program, is really intended for broadcast announcements when you're not really anticipating, or desiring, a lot of conversation about the announcement then and there.

4. Training Center: Web conferencing is the way you get back in a classroom without leaving your office or home office. Over these early years of web conferencing development, users have found that there are things standard to training sessions that don't necessarily occur in meetings. So WebEx and other vendors have developed web conferencing functions devoted to delivering training. This is a very innovative application of web conferencing

strategy; after we look at an overview of the features, interfaces, and benefits of the other centers, we will take a very close look at Training Center.

5. Business Exchange: Last, and although not a web conferencing feature per se, WebEx does have a product called Business Exchange which is a virtual office functionality to allow synchronous and asynchronous communications between people. It's like a giant filing cabinet for everything you want to keep organized in your digital life. As with most other vendors who integrate their web conferencing products to run with Outlook or perhaps Lotus Notes to allow users to integrate their web conferencing use with their other files or their calendars, so does WebEx. Business Exchange is simply another option for helping people organize and manage their files.

Online Meetings

All web conferencing in general evolved from the desire to hold meetings remotely. In general what's occurring in a virtual meeting is that all of the participants are sharing and viewing all of the same data, information, or pictures at the same time and are able to talk about it, annotate it, make notes about it, change it, or do just about anything else they could do with the data if they were in the same room with the other participants. Let's take a more detailed look at the product.

When you first enter a meeting, you will see a screen that looks like the one in Figures 5.4 and 5.5.

You'll find after working with WebEx's Meeting Center, or any of the other solutions you might try, that the fear of completely destroying either everything on your desktop or everyone on your enterprise-wide network will dissipate quickly. There's not too much you can break through the user interfaces and this will be true for all the products we look at, so we won't be giving a button-by-button description of them all.

 The main thing about all of this is that once you've chosen a solution, implemented it, and distributed it, you have to give people time and opportunity to practice with it.

Figure 5.4. The picture below is of the left upper side of a typical WebEx meeting screen. The area where the sales figures are displayed is the whiteboard area and in this case, a PowerPoint presentation has been imported into it for everyone to see. Above the whiteboard are the pull-down menus for the various file commands available in Meeting Center as well as icons that depict functionality. Holding the mouse over each icon will reveal its function as is typical with Windows software.

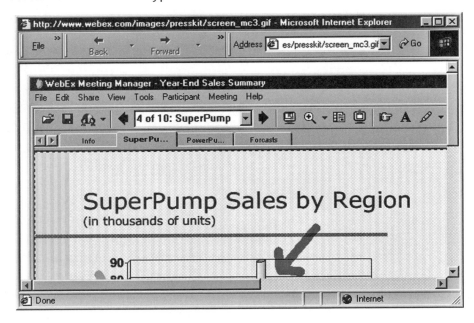

The products tend to be well designed and very intuitive, and because it's all supposed to behave the way people behave when they get together, people should be able to go with their instincts and be successful with the software(s). And they will, too, as soon as they've had a chance to play with it.

Product Features and Benefits

WebEx Meeting Center is a fully hosted system. It's accessible from any desktop, laptop, or wireless system and it will be able to transport any software program you are using to other meeting participants

Figure 5.5. WebEx Meeting Center.

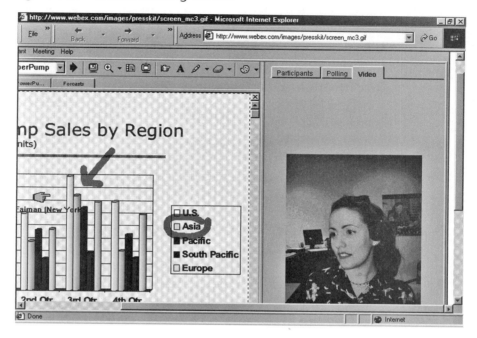

whether they are running that particular software or not on their own desktops. It needs only access to the web and a browser and you are there no matter where you actually may be.

WebEx's Meeting Center has a great deal to offer users in the realm of presentation sharing. The term *presentation sharing* refers to the fact that you can import anything into the meeting that you need on the fly. Applications, pictures, diagrams, charts, or PowerPoint presentations don't have to be downloaded to participants in order for them to see them. You simply open up a file on your own PC and everyone will see what you are looking at too. In addition, the host can take you on his magic carpet around the Internet and visit any webpage. As an added benefit, nothing that you use or see or edit during a meeting is saved at your desktop or on your network unless such permission is specifically granted during the meeting.

Why does this matter? It matters because if data or applications were stored and recorded at the network level when you wanted them to be, they could also be stored and recorded at the network level when you didn't want them to be. WebEx's strategy makes sure that nothing is saved to a network without express permission. Once saved, participants can edit, change file type, annotate, and so on.

Within the Meeting Center, remote control of a participant's system (with their permission of course) can be granted to the host in order to lend assistance on the fly. Remote management of the PC is a feature found in a lot of the systems we looked at, but not all of them allow it from the Meeting Center as opposed to whatever they are calling their support spaces. This feature could come in handy if the host were trying to make a point and a participant was having trouble following along on his screen. The host could access the participant's machine and take him to whatever page or file he needed to be at to follow along. It's the virtual answer to the question, "Hey . . . what page are we on?"

Meeting Center supports video with a PC camera. Again, this can be done on the fly; the host can let others share their video images, but it's not possible (yet) for there to be split screen or multi-point video in a single meeting. We're sure they are working on that even though video is not a big part of the WebEx collaboration story.

Providing Service and Support

OnCall is a customer service solution that allows customer service personnel to try to put the "person" back in "personnel." Remembering that all web conferencing is about collaboration, service and support solutions are focused on support being provided to people by people in ways that people are comfortable with. These solutions enable your support to literally get inside the customer's systems, whatever that system happens to be, and work with him to isolate and then, hopefully fix, the problem. Heck, people might actually start to enjoy having their computer crash. OK, doubtful. But being able to play along is infinitely more interesting than being put on hold for twenty minutes while someone in a far-off land (these days, literally) tries to reproduce your problem.

Built-In Security

Not surprisingly, a lot of the features and benefits of WebEx's customer service solution have to do with security, one of which is Agent Authentication, which allows you to be sure that the customer service rep is who she says she is and that she's authorized to play in your yard (see Figure 5.6).

Broadcast Announcements

If you need to make a big announcement to a very large audience who could be watching and listening from anywhere in the world, then WebEx Onstage could be a big help.

Figure 5.6. Demonstrates what's possible with OnCall. The user's desktop is displayed on the Support Center operator's screen along with the contents of the PC so that the problem at hand can be identified and fixed.

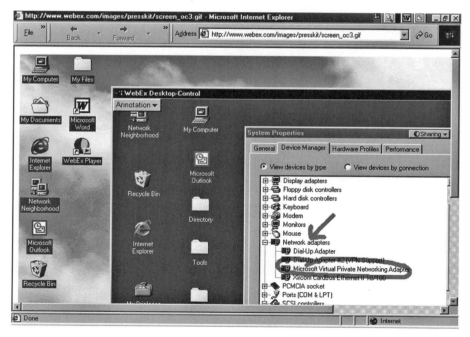

Onstage is also browser based, so there's absolutely no limit to how many people can attend your broadcast. It has a couple of things going in it that differ from smaller group meeting scenarios, among which are its ability to allow for multiple presenters who may be in different locations themselves, manage access across a larger number of participants, and also get feedback about the announcement or conduct Q&As in real time regardless of how many people are out there. And you can record your event while it's going on so that it can be viewed and edited afterwards. In addition to travel savings, these recording and reusing savings can add up too.

Other features that are relevant to large events include the ability to announce your event using customized emails to an enormous distribution list that is fully integrated with the software. Managing your distribution list is one of the functions of Business Exchange that is integrated with the other centers (see Figure 5.7).

Figure 5.7. In this screen shot of OnStage, a presentation is being given in the whiteboard section of the screen while a Q&A is actively on-going between the presenter and all the participants.

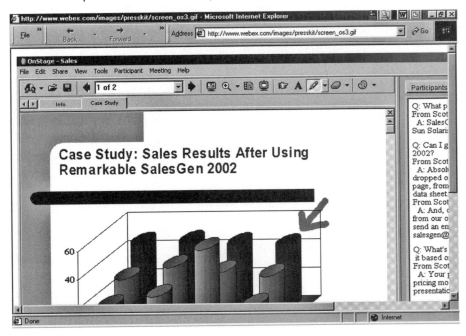

Enrollment functions are included with OnStage that both capture information about enrollees and also block enrollment requests as the host sees fit.

Training Delivery

In talking to any of the representatives from the various web conferencing and accessory vendors that we spoke to while researching this book, one thing became abundantly clear. That is that right now, the most common uses of web conferencing are external communications types of uses: meetings, announcements, and sales oriented utilization.

Mr. Praful Shah, VP of Strategic Communications for WebEx, put it best when he talked about the fact that we are still in the infancy of visual and collaborative communications and that it will be some time before people are more comfortable exchanging all sorts of information digitally, beyond just visual information. Widespread adaptation of web conferencing that is fully leveraged will take some time for people. But the thing that people will really latch on to when they start to become more familiar and comfortable with web conferencing will be its tremendous potential to positively enhance training and educational efforts of all kinds.

In terms of general functionality, Training Center allows all of the sharing and annotating capabilities of all kinds of files. And as with the other centers, it integrates with whatever mechanism you choose for audio conferencing, permits the integration of video, and also enables record and playback of training sessions.

Because doing training also requires administrative features like registering attendees, getting authorization to enroll them, tracking attendees' participation in various training courses you offer, and, of course, doing billing, Training Center is the only one of the WebEx centers fully integrated with Microsoft Outlook or Lotus Notes or other popular document management programs. WebEx wisely recognized that, at least for now, more people are running Outlook. What this integration allows is that when a person registers for a session, that session is automatically entered into his Outlook calendar along with the information about how he will access the training session, and so on.

The Outlook integration allows the company using WebEx Training Center to invite people to training sessions in a targeted marketing fashion, to easily communicate with their participants, and to track their use of their training products. This doesn't mean that you can't participate in training sessions run on Training Center if you don't have Outlook. It just means that the administrative and other tasks associated with your training won't be done automatically or electronically.

Delivering training with web conferencing requires the ability to share with participants. It's also important that you be able to have multiple panelists or instructors to deliver the course collaboratively. Other must-have features include testing and grading where the answers are shared instantaneously or not depending on instructor preference, questions and answers, and polling capabilities. These functions are called instant feedback functions and allow everyone to see how everyone else is doing, just as occurs in a live classroom.

In WebEx Training Center they have a threaded Q&A which appears as a form of a threaded chat in which a participant's question and the answer to it appear concurrently. The fact that the Q&A is threaded means that everyone can see the progression of questions to answers and how they lead to other questions. A regular chat, or one that just occurs privately between the instructor and a student or between students, is also supported. But as in a real classroom, it's up to the instructor whether or not she'll let students chat among themselves or only with her.

Another important feature is the ability to conduct multiple, simultaneous breakout sessions that allow participants to collaborate in teams on remote applications or documents, and the instructor(s) can see what they are all doing and/or work with individual groups at different times.

Figure 5.8 depicts a lot of what Training Center offers in a single view. Starting on the left-hand side of the picture, in the field that would commonly comprise the whiteboard area, we see that a desktop version of Outlook is provided which, in this case, is telling the owner that he's scheduled for this training session. If he were to click on the line item about the training session, he'd see the details for joining the course. The whiteboard area is where all files that are

Figure 5.8. A single view of Training Center.

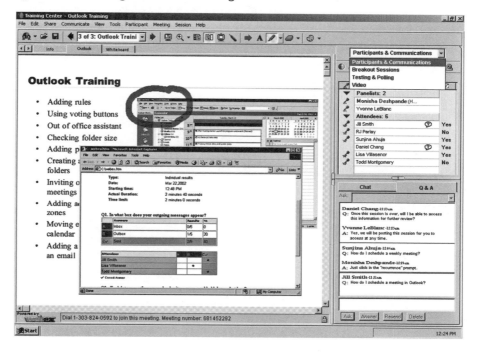

brought into the training session are viewed, where annotation of that data takes place, or where people can brainstorm about things using the various writing or drawing tools provided in the software.

The window overlaying the Outlook view is an example of what the instant feedback would look like within a training session, while the tool bars at the top are fully familiar to anyone who works with any kind of Windows applications. All of the tools in the bar closest to the main screen (the pictogram tools) provide a description of their functionality when you hold a mouse over them, the same as would occur in any Windows program. And the file, edit, share, communicate, and so on tools above the pictograms are standard pull-down menus.

Look over at the right side of this screen shot and you'll see other functionality depicted. The first pull-down menu in which participants and communications is highlighted shows that there are two instructors and six participants. In this example, Monisha is also the host of this particular class, so it is she who controls who has what

Case Study

Countrywide Home Loans uses WebEx for its training in its wholesale lending division. These are the folks who work directly with mortgage brokers to sell and service loans. The financial professionals who staff each office must remain knowledgeable about the company's many products and processes, so consequently, the division has a long history of investment in employee training.

This commitment to training had, of course, a downside. That was that employees from all over the country had to fly to, and stay at, facilities in California, Texas, and Illinois, sometimes for a week or more at a time. According to Ron Schneider, First VP of training and performance development for this division, the costs of the training were very high, especially as Countrywide continued to grow. So they needed to develop, in his words, ". . . more training while maintaining a superior training product but at a lesser cost."

Countrywide Home Loans found out that another of Countrywide's divisions (there are a few under the Countrywide Credit Industries which is the parent company) was using WebEx's Meeting Center product for both meetings and training. As we pointed out before, this was not an unusual use of Meeting Center and is the thing (i.e., customer demand) that led to a dedicated Training Center product.

They performance tested Training Center extensively to make sure that WebEx could provide the framework they required to support the training they needed and wanted. Their testing and assessment must have been good because today, all of Countrywide's training takes place over the Internet where trainers and trainees alike do no more traveling than to a common URL.

One training application that has seen enormous benefit, according to Countrywide, is in their orientation training. Before implementing training via the Web, each branch did their own orientation training and the results, according to corporate, were very inconsistent. Now, all new hires meet two hours per day for five days in a web training in which they all get the same message about the company in the same way.

capabilities. In addition to the host, there can be people called panelists who are sort of co-facilitators of the course and who will have whatever communicative privileges the host allows them.

As you can see, the six participants can indicate that they have questions, and when they send those questions, the panelists can answer them in the same thread as we described before. You'll also note that each participant has a microphone icon next to his or her name. If a participant clicks on their microphone, the panelists can see that and it indicates that person has something to say. Although not depicted in this view, there is also a way for participants to raise their hands in order to ask a question verbally, via the Q&A or in a chat that (probably) would be private between him and the instructor.

Figure 5.9 shows the screen when the video capability is turned on for either the host, another panelist, or perhaps one of the participants in order to show the rest of the people in the class what is being talked about.

Figure 5.9. Video Capability Screen.

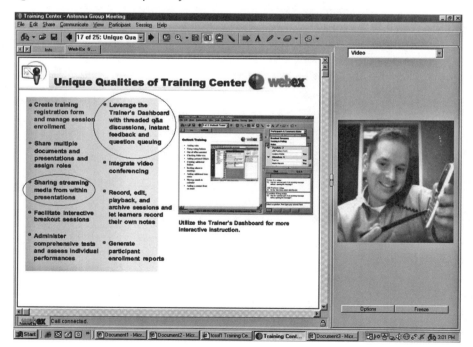

Figure 5.10 demonstrates an annotation of the slide being projected in the whiteboard part of the screen. The annotation is occurring in real time, which is referred to as "on the fly" annotation. In the upper right-hand corner of the slide window, the various tools that can be used to annotate are presented.

On the right-hand side of this figure, we see the various communications icons that all the participants have at their disposal to raise their hand, and so on. We can also see who's currently speaking (Sara, the instructor) and that she is also conducting a Q&A with participants.

What is not depicted in these figures, but it's fun functionality that some vendors are offering, are "emoticons." These are ways for participants to let the instructor and other participants know what they are feeling, not just what they are thinking. Examples are icons that depict laughter, applause, confusion, info coming too fast or too slow, and so on.

Figure 5.10. Projecting a slide for annotation in the whiteboard.

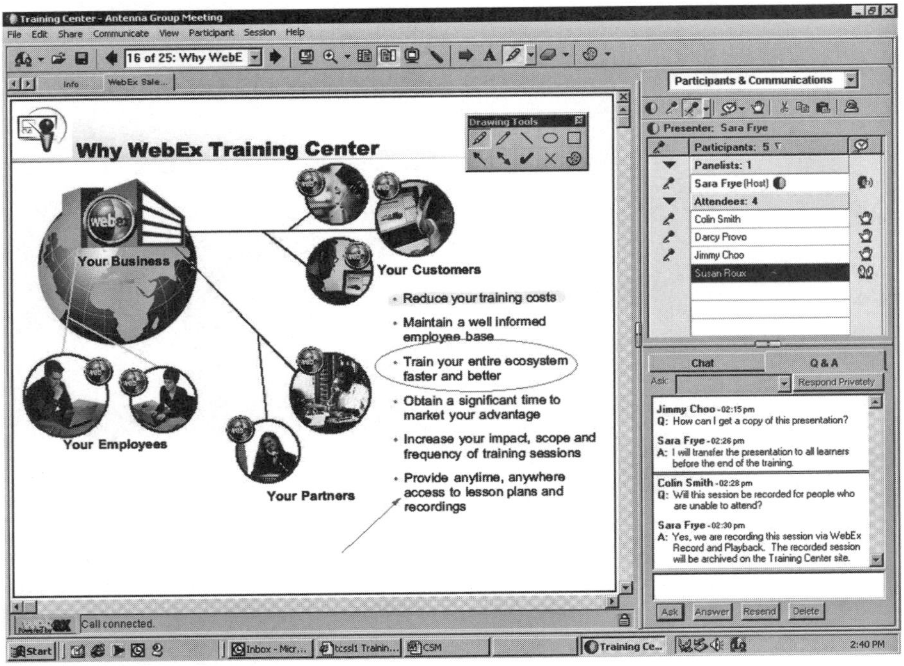

Figure 5.11 shows the results of a poll that was given during the course. The poll question is indicated, along with the correct answer, and the percentage of folks who chose each answer presented as both the numerical and as a bar graph. What's different about a poll versus a test is that the responses to a test wouldn't be shared unless the instructor chose to, but a poll is always shared. Also the entire test time would elapse before the tests were checked where the answers to a poll are posted immediately. As with all other content in web conferencing, tests and polls can be created beforehand and simply called up by the instructor when she's ready to administer them. Test questions can be multiple choice with one answer, multiple choice where more than one answer is permitted, and/or fill in the blank-type questions.

In short, this technology will do everything that people want (or in the case of tests, don't want) to do in a class.

Figure 5.11. Sample polling results view.

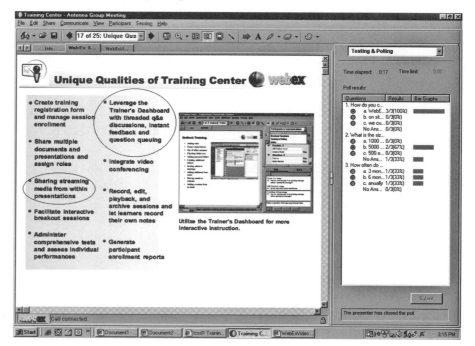

Interwise ECP—Another Way to Look at General Business Communication

Interwise, a vendor that competes with WebEx, looked at the world of web conferencing slightly differently than WebEx. They, too, think that the full plate of web conferencing capabilities should be both ubiquitous and accessible from anywhere, but they decided that the presentation of the capabilities should be from a single viewpoint. So Interwise created the Enterprise Communications Platform (ECP), which is a single, fully integrated web-based platform. What this means for those of us who speak English first and technology second is that the five different collaboration tools that Interwise offers, which they call "Modes," all look basically the same (other than customization by users and user organizations), are all available at a single price per year for up to three hundred users, and are all very scalable to support access by just a few people or literally thousands of people depending on the mode you're using.

Like WebEx, Interwise is hosted on a dedicated and distributed server infrastructure that they call the Interwise Expressway. Expressway supports the Interwise Communications Center, which is the heart of how the modes work and how they are distributed.

ECP is different from most other general web conferencing providers in that its voice integration is strictly Voice Over IP (VOIP). So that means that to use this system, you'll need a quality set of speakers and microphone, or if you don't want to disturb the people around you, a really good headset.

To run Interwise ECP you also need their software, which is available as a downloaded Interwise application or as a Java applet. WebEx doesn't require any special software download to run. With its tightly integrated strategy, its dedication to delivering quality voice capability with its web conferencing Modes, and its close relationship with Microsoft Outlook to enhance aspects of some of its Modes, ECP supports Windows only.

So to sum up, the Interwise strategy for web conferencing looks like Figure 5.12. Figure 5.12 denotes Interwise's attempt to fill in the gap between email—phone communications and in-person interac-

Figure 5.12. Interwise strategy for web conferencing.

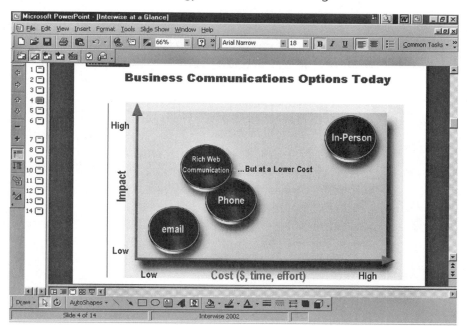

tion. They did this by creating what they call a Rich Web Communication that incorporates the best features of web conferencing with phone and email capabilities in order to have high impact, but low cost, collaboration among people. In their worldview, this approach means less hassles for technical staff who only have to support one platform and application, not many. ECP is a single application, a single interface,* and a single price point for access to everything in the product. Interwise believes that this approach is more in line with how people actually communicate.

Let's look at what comprises the five Modes and additional features of ECP.

---

*Single interface in this context means that even though there are different functions for each of Interwise's web conferencing Modes, they all sort of look the same to the user.

iMeeting

We started with the meeting platform when discussing WebEx, and it's a logical place to start here too. iMeeting is meant to foster collaboration and knowledge exchange among small workgroups over the Web, whether they be scheduled in advance or on the fly.

To optimize the user's experience with iMeeting, it uses a single interface and toolset that is meant to mirror, exactly, the sorts of things that people do in face-to-face meetings. You can initiate and access iMeetings directly from Outlook or from the Interwise Communications Center, create content on the fly (by pulling it from wherever it resides on your network, desktop, or on the Web), and you can also use five-way video conferencing. Naturally you can have more than five people at a meeting, but only five can project video at any one time. Note also that the video will stream only one image; if there are two to four others, they will appear as still shots. The moderator of the meeting can assign whose video is streaming when (see Figure 5.13). (Note: In WebEx's lexicon, "moderator" is "host." We point this out so you know that the various vendors use different terminology for the same things . . . another reason why we felt the need to write this book.)

iMeetings can be recorded, edited, protected, and reused. These functions are all part of the Interwise Expressway, which really is the main administrative point of the product. You should note that iMeeting, therefore, can take place as live meetings or as on-demand events. In other words, if there were a meeting and you couldn't attend it when it was actually occurring, you could access it later to see what went on.

Unlike the other modes we'll look at, iMeetings are more democratic in so far as how it's determined who gets to speak. In iMeetings all attendees enjoy equal speaking rights and control over materials presentation. When speaking, a participant also has control over the discussion, what's being viewed on screen, where the participants are taken on the Net, and whose video is streaming, if any. This is accomplished because the participants indicate that they have something to contribute and the software acknowledges and queues their requests in the order received automatically. Unlike face-to-face meetings, you

Figure 5.13. Video streaming with Interwise.

can't actually interrupt someone else, but you can certainly try! We think this is adorably human.

Two other features worth noting are that iMeetings are automatically recorded so you can document the results of your discussion and share relevant segments with those unable to attend. And snapshots of anything on the whiteboard can be taken by anyone and saved to any location for use later. Interwise has available, too, a Digital Rights Management tool as part of the Expressway that administrates control of downloading, recording, or capturing functions.

iCast

This mode is for live or recorded events broadcast via the Web to thousands of geographically distributed participants. iCasts are intended for things like product launches, marketing announcements, product or competitive updates, "town hall meetings," and things of that ilk. The tools and interface are designed to provide the sorts of things you would commonly associate with such events (see Figure 5.14).

The thing that Interwise is most focused on with iCast is consistency of message—that everyone around the world with access to the iCast gets the same message in every way, shape, and form. And the interface has in mind that there could be thousands of people involved at once.

So, for instance, the product offers a Stadium Participant View where participants become visible in the arena-style view as they come forward to ask questions. The participants don't have to all be in the same place; each is represented by an icon. The moderator, who in this mode is controlling who sees what and who is speaking, has available to him a Search the Crowd capability that allows him to instantly seek and select specific individuals by their associated icon. This is made possible because, like iMeetings, iCasts are accessible through Outlook

Figure 5.14. An overview of iCast.

and the ICC; doing it this way allows for capturing of registration information and who is accessing iCast from where so that the icons can be preassigned when a person registers. Then that icon will appear on the moderator's list when that person comes online to the iCast.

iCasts are brandable, so each event can be customized with logos, hyperlinks, and preaddressed email. The moderator can use video that is available via a USB camera and no additional video cards. And this software sports a feature of Intelligent Video Streaming that withholds video from participants who lack the bandwidth to support it so that they will not have annoying interruptions.

Last, you can use iCast for live broadcasts or recorded programs that can be downloaded, streamed, or made available through a portal on your website. If you wish, these recorded offerings can be hosted live so that you can have that real-time feeling for an event that happened previously.

iMentoring

Going from the greatest number of people mode, iCast, to the smallest number mode with Interwise is called iMentoring, which is designed for very small groups, or even one-on-one interaction, problem solving, and skills transfer.

The most unusual characteristic of this Mode is called Over the Shoulder, which is exactly what it sounds like. It's the ability of the moderator to view and control a participant's desktop for skills building and problem solving. If the person or people being mentored are having trouble following along, this feature allows the mentor to show them what she's talking about. And while this mode is available as a live occurrence or one that is recordable, it is most effective as a live tool because otherwise, why wouldn't you just run a meeting for people to view later? (See Figure 5.15.)

You can schedule an iMentoring event in advance or also access it on the fly when a problem comes up. The only possible difficulty we see with this model is that since Interwise is a single platform solution requiring participants to have either their software or the Java applet, it might be lacking a bit in the customer service department if the

Figure 5.15. Mentoring at a glance.

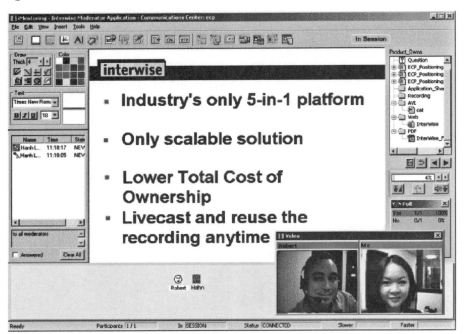

customer in question doesn't have immediate access to those down-loadable programs. This is just something to keep in mind.

iClass

iClass is for leader-led learning. There are other learning models that we'll examine in Chapter Seven, but leader-led learning is, as the term implies, led by a live person during a real-time session. Note that this mode, like all the others, is recordable and reusable. In this mode, recordability has several applications, not the least of which is the ability to reuse a class and create an additional revenue stream. But keep in mind that some things are not as effective as recorded events where a person is viewing them in isolation. Remember that the whole point of web conferencing is collaboration; you can't collaborate with a tape. So we think that even though recordable functionality abounds, it's not really the essence or even value of what web conferencing modes have to offer, especially in educationally focused formats like iClass.

Interwise, like WebEx before it, seems to believe as we do that when web conferencing moves beyond the one-to-many or meeting comfort zones of people using it, that it will move next most naturally into our training lives. As such, they put a lot of effort into developing this mode of their product (see Figure 5.16).

Among these features are the ability to deliver content in Microsoft OfficeSuite documents, as Acrobat files or as Flash files. You can also deliver CBT (computer-based training) courses including prerecorded video clips and Interwise recordings from previous sessions integrated into the current class. The moderator can utilize the full scope of the Internet by taking the class wherever she'd like, send documents intended to be handouts to the participants either before

Figure 5.16. iClass overview screen and capability.

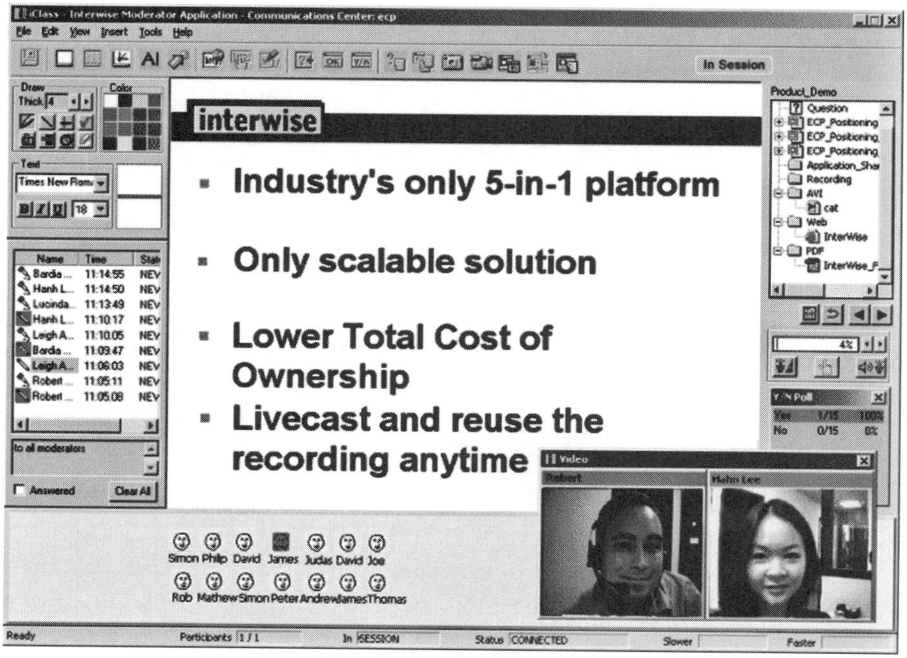

or during the class that they can keep in a desktop file or print, and she can enable video still picture or streaming video (one at a time, up to five total at a time) so that people can see each other or perhaps an object under discussion.

Breakout sessions and Over the Shoulder functionality are also present in iClass, as is the ability to do yes/no polling, administer tests and quizzes, get real-time assessments, acknowledge raised hands, and also for the instructor to get anonymous feedback from students. As an ex-teacher, Liz isn't sure about this last one, but it's there, like it or not.

iClass also sports a self-exercise mode that enables study time for participants to review materials or prepare for written or verbal exams during class time. The instructor can have teacher assistants present to help with one-to-one interaction or specific parts of the class content; branding is also available that allows emphasis of a company logo or branded buttons for email messages and hyperlinks within the "classroom."

A few features that all you instructor types out there in particular might like are that iClass offers a Lesson Template Builder that enables creation of standard agenda materials quickly and easily. It also sports an Office Hours functionality that engenders after-class interaction among participants and the instructor; the page includes customizable buttons that create email templates and URLs for on-demand follow-up. Last, instructors can integrate Interwise's Knowledge Nuggets™ which are knowledge repositories built by Interwise ECP based on recorded segments of information from busy subject experts who can't be at every class, but who can record their material to be available to anyone authorized to use them. (Sort of how you never actually get the full professors teaching the courses at all those high-priced Ivy League and Pac Ten schools anymore.) These recordings can be edited, protected, reused, or distributed for multiple purposes at any time.

iSeminar

Designed to fit below the numerical capabilities of iCast, and without the necessarily participatory features of iClass or iMeeting, but definitely designed to reach more people at a time than iMentoring,

Interwise offers iSeminar. This mode is specifically for live or recorded seminar-style events delivered via the Web for hundreds, not thousands, of geographically dispersed participants. They are intended for high-level learning, new product orientations, marketing announcements, lead generation programs, product or service seminars, competitive and press/analyst briefings, and so on.

A big draw to iSeminar is its branding capabilities—the ability to use the software to make the statement you wish with customizable buttons for logos, URLs, and automatic email. Figure 5.17 represents such a branded iSeminar offering from the Harvard Business School.

As with the other Interwise modes, what it lacks in support for platforms other than Windows or the inability to support every application in the world seamlessly, it makes amends for with its single platform approach of the Interwise Communications Center running

Figure 5.17. Branding your out-going messages and face to the world.

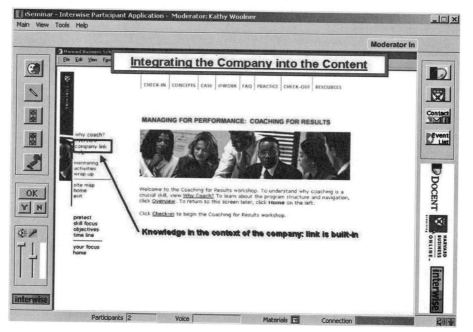

on the Expressway, which enables almost limitless scalability (growth potential) and the ability of people regardless of their location, bandwidth, or connection speed to experience optimum performance of the software, including VOIP integration for the program that they are attending. There is good and bad in everything.

In terms of the features of this mode that are specific to seminar delivery, there are a couple that do stand out. Among them, the facilitator can view up to two hundred participants without scrolling. This seems a bit fantastic, but it goes back to the fact that participants are assigned icons that we mentioned before. What the facilitator is actually seeing is a list of icons and their associated participants. Up to two-hundred of these can be seen on screen at once and that's why no scrolling is required. The facilitator can also put polls and surveys out for all to see and respond to as well as see the results quickly and easily. She can have an unlimited number of assistant moderators and she can utilize both application sharing and instant assessment tools that she either prepares in advance or creates on the fly. Last, iSeminars are automatically recorded so they can be shared with those unable to attend.

Managing Projects with Web Conferencing

Chapter
6

When people think about collaboration in a business context, it's not unusual for them to think about it in terms of collaboration on projects—what is commonly called project management. So it's quite logical that there would be room in the web conferencing world for at least one product that was specifically built with project management in mind. We found such a product called eRoom.

eRoom is differentiated by its philosophy about collaboration in projects within the realm of web conferencing because it is almost entirely an asynchronous solution as opposed to all of the other products we'll examine which are synchronous, or real-time, communication models.

The eRoom Way

The researchers and analysts at the Gartner Group believe that the most benefits of collaborative software are realized when people and processes intersect.

The folks who bring eRoom into the world agree with these sentiments wholeheartedly, and that's why their web conferencing solution is 85 percent asynchronous—designed to be used most effectively when all or any number of people involved in a project are not in the same cyber-place at the same time. The software is all about project management and the organization of information and data. Only about 15 percent of it has any applicability to real-time meetings or online, live collaboration. To boot, that 15 percent is rudimentary in its capabilities to support web meetings. In other words, all the bells and whistles of eRoom are about managing the complexity of any size project because people, complex animals that we are, just love to complicate things.

Figures 6.1 to 6.3 demonstrate the evolution of project complexity that led eRoom to set their product up as they did.

As these diagrams demonstrate, what works for a transaction between two entities, as in the example in Figure 6.1 between a supplier and an enterprise, will not work as soon as you get people involved. People involvement means approval processes, questions, negotiation, change, and so on. And as demonstrated by Figure 6.3, get folks outside of your organization involved too and the whole thing becomes a spider's web of intrigue worthy of Hitchcock. Collaborative processes are dynamic, ever changing, complex, and they build upon one another as the collaboration or project moves forward. Further, although a project will have a beginning point and a targeted ending point, it's a road that, like the one to Hell, is littered

Figure 6.1. Collaboration is dynamic.

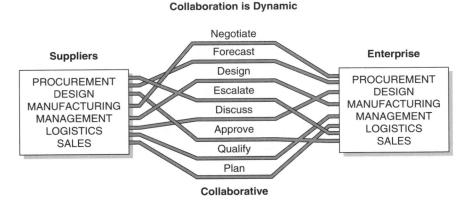

Figure 6.2. External collaboration is even more dynamic.

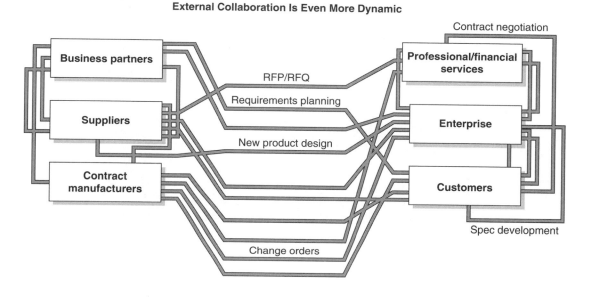

External Collaboration Is Even More Dynamic

Figure 6.3. The people, processes, and tools to get the work done.

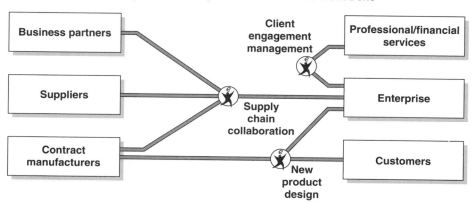

The People, Processes, and Tools to Get the Work Done

with good intentions. What's required in reality is not only a way to effectively collaborate with remote teams and resources, but also a way to keep things organized without losing any of the dynamic creative energy of the participants that will be, ultimately, the reason for success (hopefully) of the project.

So, eRoom looked at the need to create a web space for dynamic collaboration that is organized, and they hit upon what they call the eRoom Digital Workplace (see Figure 6.4).

The eRoom Digital Workplace is a flexible, web-based workplace that enables distributed teams to work together both cross-functionally and across the firewalls of other organizations. If you look at the different ways that dynamic collaboration is represented by Figure 6.3 and then in Figure 6.4, you'll see that all the same entities are represented, but in Figure 6.4, the communication, collaboration, interaction, and transactions between them are not free flow but rather are organized and stored in these things called eRooms.

Figure 6.4. eRoom Digital Workplace.

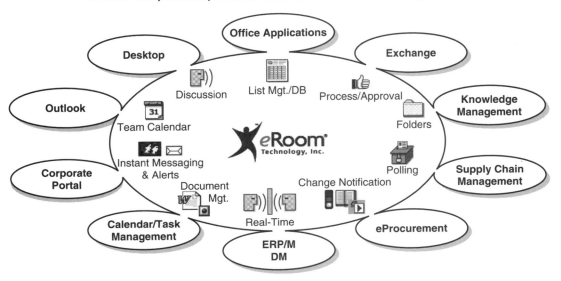

With Apologies to Virginia Woolf: An eRoom of One's Own

An eRoom by definition is the logical organization of information created, maintained, and managed precisely as people choose to use it. Content is captured in eRooms and then it is archived, indexed, and disseminated. There can be a small number of eRooms created for a small project, or a practically unlimited number for a very large project. They are flexible and scalable; there is no limit to the number of folders you can create within a room or how many eRooms/folders can be nested one into another. Figure 6.4 is a visual representation of the capabilities of the eRoom Digital Workplace.

As you can see from this figure, eRooms are built to support standard business applications such as Word, PowerPoint, and Excel as well as eCommerce- and eProcurement-type Process applications (self-generated or off-the-shelf). It also supports whatever methods you use or create for Knowledge Management systems and Supply Management systems. eRoom also has the ability to share applications and data directly from one desktop to another, or to manage the content of one's desktop. Further, eRooms can be created, maintained, and accessed from a portal environment by which you allow access to certain data/information by your internal staff or an external constituency (with security provisions for both, of course).

To no one's surprise, eRooms can also be fully integrated with any calendar/task/document management system.

Within all of this support for applications, strategies, paradigms, models, techniques and so on comes the whole range of functionality that you might use in project management. This is represented by the inner circle of functions depicted in Figure 6.4 for example, email, folders, polling, document management, instant messaging, and the like.

So eRooms might serve many different purposes. For example, in Figure 6.5 we see a visual collaboration eRoom in which a new product design is being shared with other members of project team.

On the left-hand side of this eRoom, we see that this project team has created a whole host of eRooms for the Spacely Sprocket project.

Figure 6.5. Visual collaboration.

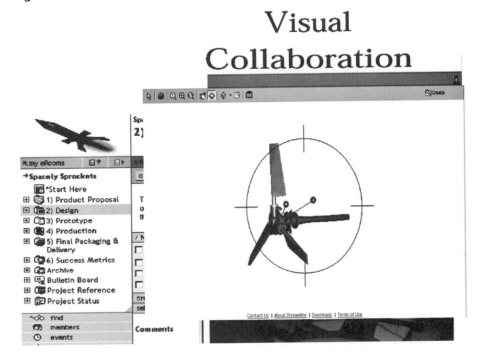

One of these eRooms is a series of folders dedicated to the design of the product, and it's from there that this diagram originated.

Then Figure 6.6 shows an editorial comment made by a member of the team. This comment will be viewed by everyone on the team who checks that folder or, if it's a question that requires everyone's attention, each member of the team will get an email or instant message telling them there's something in the design eRoom that requires their attention. The basis of all of this type of collaboration is that each person's input builds upon the previous input, but it doesn't have to occur in real time. If you are the member of the team in Colorado who put up the original drawing, it could be someone on your team in Sydney, Australia, who put up the comment, likely while you were sleeping.

Figure 6.6. Visual collaboration you can build on.

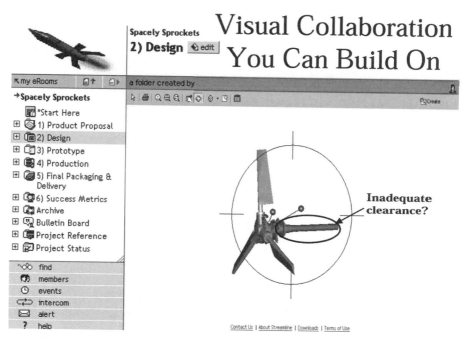

As we'll see in a few moments, eRoom chose not only a particular design strategy for its Digital Workplace, it also focused on supporting vertical business relationships (see Figure 6.7).

eRoom can help manufacturers align supply and demand signals across the value chain. By providing a workspace for sharing up-to-the-minute demand forecasts, suppliers can respond to demand changes based upon what they are able to commit. Through a series of collaborative interactions, the manufacturer and supplier are able to get consensus on delivery requirements, effectively aligning supply and demand. This application is often used together with a traditional supply chain management application for collaborating around exceptions such as supply stock outs and demand spikes.

Figure 6.7. Forecast/Inventory collaboration.

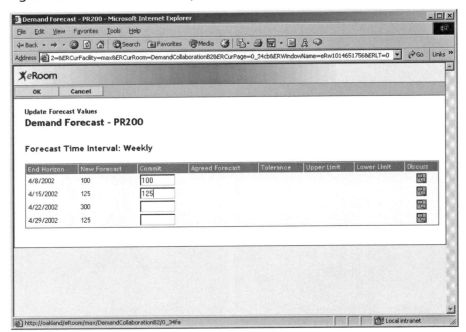

The ability to do these sorts of things in eRooms differs from, for example, just sending emails back and forth because emails are simply linear communication. True, one email can lead to another and so on, and the string of emails about a subject can be easily enough followed, but it's going to be a long string. Performing the kind of supply/demand jobs as described earlier is much easier if all of the information about any part of the process is kept in its own eRoom and can be viewed singly or as part of the whole. It's the difference between collaborative communication and back-and-forth communication.

And in yet another example of how eRooms are used to manage projects, Figure 6.8 is a picture of how the HP/Compaq merger was managed. According to HP's Webb McKinney, President, Business Customer Organization, "This (eRoom structure) was the nerve center of all of the information. Everyone involved with the integration kept the information here and accessed the information here." This

Figure 6.8. Structured approval processes.

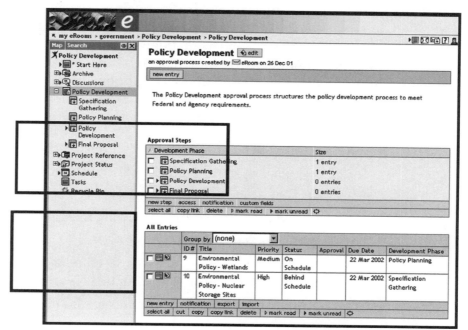

integration project consisted of (in eRoom lingo) 500,000 work-hours spent in merger eRooms, 2,600 folders, and 10,000+ files. Looking at the figure should give you an idea of the intricacies and depth of project information that can be created.

How Do They Manage All That?

The asynchronous design of eRoom was not due to any technical limitations as we mentioned; it was based on a practical assumption by eRoom that people in a large-scale distributed team are working independently most of the time and they are working across geographies, time zones, and platforms. So someone will change a document, as with the Spacely Sprocket example, and someone else will add something to a discussion thread and then others will join in. All of this occurs across a span of time against specific goals or milestones for a project.

eRoom also features many of the same attributes as you'd expect from classic, synchronous web conferencing technology. The rudimentary synchronous attributes of the product are real-time chat, document sharing, and whiteboarding. As for the structure of the product, eRoom has a few preloaded templates, but for the most part it is ad hoc all the way with lots of options to impose structure, but that structure is entirely user driven.

Additional product features are:

- The ability to create intricate or simple nested folders
- A workplace map navigation not unlike a site map on a website
- Drag and drop file transfer
- Threaded discussions (and archiving to beat the band)
- Project calendar templates
- Personalized task summaries (so each person can see what the whole team is doing and/or what he is responsible for)
- The ability to do keyword searches across multiple eRooms
- Support for multistep approval processes
- Full accessibility via your browser

Technologically speaking, eRoom's Digital Workplace is end-user configurable, which means that each Project Manager can configure the eRooms for her project to look exactly as she wishes. The workplace is also seamless across firewalls. This means that regardless of what kind of firewall protection your organization is using to protect itself and its data, you'll be able to set up eRoom on your network to work with your firewalls. It's designed to work with your existing databases and applications. As for actual management by real people on real projects, eRoom structures people as follows:

- Administrator has carte blanche (full permission and access) to do anything regarding the structure and content of eRooms created around a given project or projects.

- Coordinator can invite other people (members) into the eRoom, create and edit documents, and give out permission to do so to others.

- Member is a knowledge worker in an eRoom or eRooms (as made accessible by the administrator) with basic abilities to create, edit, and share files.

- Observer is a person with read-only access to eRoom(s) within the scope of the project.

So aside from some sensitive administrative tasks, most functionality is fully distributed and members of eRooms can get nightly batched-based or real-time notification of updates to all of the eRooms and content within their area of responsibility. There are also audit trails within the product for tracking modifications and who made them over the life of a project. Permission to view, change, or do anything else you can think of with information can be assigned for a whole room or sections of a room; different people can have different permissions at different times, and these permissions can be adjusted as need be.

The structure of the product for the management of projects mirrors the face-to-face hierarchy that most people are used to in which people higher up the corporate ladder have access to more information and permission to manipulate it more.

Of Templates, Databases, and Other Matters of Import

There are databases and templates that are part and parcel of eRoom that the users can use as is or customize to meet their needs. This customization can be done for an entire project that uses 1,000 eRooms or any subset of the eRooms of a project. And it's part of this design that allows for any kind of file that you might have to use within a project to be accessed, stored, and shared as an extension of the eRoom in which you place it. This is all made possible because eRoom is what is referred to as file agnostic, a trait shared by all of the best-of-breed web conferencing products. In eRoom's case, the environment is built in HTML and ASP,* so all eRoom interfaces can be modified the same way as you would modify a webpage. You can create links, change fonts, and customize the appearance of the user interface and brand of all of your eRooms to have whatever your organization's look and feel is.

The database objects are where the templates for the various types of documents or notes you'll use in a project reside, and the templates reflect specific types of databases that are commonly created like contacts, document libraries, issues, issue trackers, milestones and the like. One of them, for example, is a multistep approval process that can be created within the database object. A version of it might look like Figure 6.8.

Still another database template might concern itself with who has access to what in the various eRooms. Such a template might resemble this Figure 6.9.

There are other capabilities of the product such as the ability to create an inbox for each eRoom in a project with its own IP address so an entire eRoom can be cc'd on an email. This is not only a neat communications vehicle, it's another way of preserving the history of a project.

And speaking of preserving the history of a project, another of the database templates that anyone trying to manage a very large project would likely find helpful is the ability to do contextual version tracking** as demonstrated by Figure 6.10.

As you can see from the example provided in Figure 6.10, the version of any part of any data in any eRoom can be identified at the click of a mouse so that the project manager can ensure that everyone is on the same page. And would that be refreshing?

There are literally hundreds of ways to interact with eRoom for project management, even if your first time using it is after reading

---

*See terms in Chapter Four for definitions.

**Refers to the ability to track the progress of a project based on the version or revision number of the update. In other words, every time an eRoom is updated, you can save the old version with a date or a revision number (or both) so that you can always see where the project was at any given time.

Figure 6.9. Granular access controls.

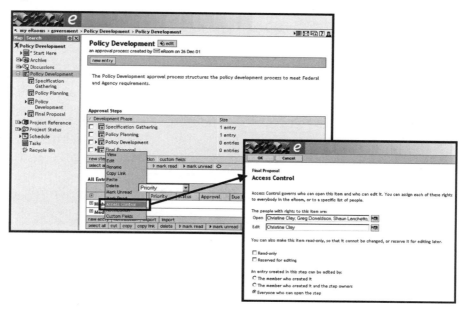

Figure 6.10. Contextual version tracking.

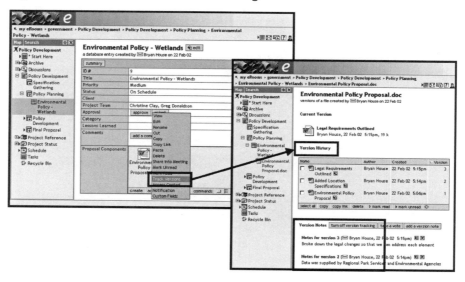

this chapter; then you should be able to appreciate the method behind the madness. In the basic design of the eRoom Digital Workplace, document management via databases is where all content is archived, indexed, and disseminated from, while the eRooms themselves, be they templates, customizations, or a mixture of both, are for capturing and presenting that content.

That said, there's only one more specific feature of eRoom that we'll make you aware of, and that's the ability to roll up information. For example, Figure 6.11 demonstrates the rolling up of tasks so that one person can see both all the tasks associated with a project and also the tasks that she's on the hook for.

As a last example, Figure 6.12 shows that anything associated with your project can be made to roll up across the eRooms in which those aspects reside.

Figure 6.11.   Task management.

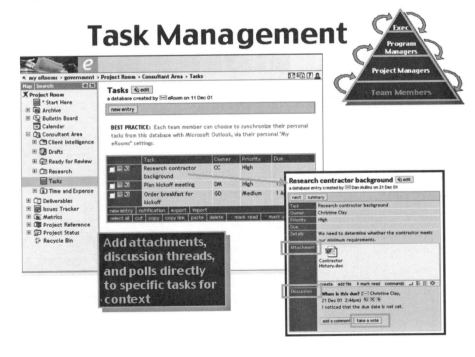

Figure 6.12.   Enterprise rollup.

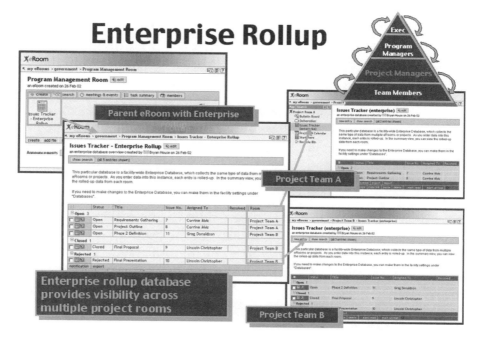

Vertical, Not Vertigo

eRoom can be used by any organization in any market, but the product has particular strengths for professional services, manufacturing, biopharmaceutical, financial services, and government. The reason for this is that these verticals tend to have ways of doing things that are particular to their vertical market, even if they are involved in different aspects within that vertical.

eRoom identified the following common requirements in each of these markets and then developed functionality in their product that is adept at fulfilling those requirements.

- Professional Services: client engagement, proposal development, project portfolio management

- Manufacturing: new product development, design collaboration, ECO (engineering change orders for the uninitiated) management, forecasting/inventory collaboration, supplier score-carding

- Biopharmaceutical: competitive intelligence/licensing, lead generation/optimization, industrial operation/sales and marketing, risk management

- Financial Services: research, deal management, M&A (mergers and acquisitions for the chronically uninitiated ☺)

- Government: contract management, policy development, program/project management, emergency response management

We thought you'd find this information useful if you happen to work at an organization that resides in one of these spaces. It's also good to know these strengths exist in the product since certainly some of the items listed under each of the bullets are also found in companies outside of these vertical markets.

Finding Your Voice—Telephony and Web Conferencing

Chapter

7

Telephony, according to the American Standard Dictionary, is the transmission of sound between distant points, especially by electronic or electrical means. Telephony is an intricate part of web conferencing because no matter how much data you can share, Internet you can surf, or control you can take over someone else's PC during a web conference, if you can't also talk to the other people on the conference, the results will be less satisfying to human beings than otherwise.

The telephone is the most logical way for voice interaction (what used to be called "talking" so why don't we just call it that now?) to occur because just about everyone you'll encounter who has a PC is also going to have a telephone (or maybe even a half dozen of them on three different lines plus a cell phone . . . like us), and is also going to know how to use them. But there are some downsides to dependence on the telephone to support talking in conjunction with web conferencing. First, what if there are a lot of people on the integrated call? Will your phone and phone network support conferencing or will you have to go to a third-party vendor to host and manage your calls? And if you do go outside, what's that going to cost? Speaking of cost, even if you can manage your telephone use on your own network, phone charges are typically billed per minute and, as we all know, it can be impossible to say with any accuracy how long a call, especially a conference call, is going to run. So, how do you plan and budget for telephone telecommunications?

Another thing to consider is if you are a small shop or a home-user and you don't have separate lines for voice and data, then you won't be able to use web conferencing technology without VOIP (Voice Over Internet Protocol).

But before you assume that we are pushing VOIP, consider these things. First, VOIP is not yet very stable, dependable, or reliable. We believe it will be all three in short order, but there are no guarantees that stability, dependability, and reliability won't come without some costs of their own—monetary, logistical, or both. On top of that, a mass transition to VOIP in your organization, regardless of size, or in your home for that matter, will demand a whole new way of looking at standard PC equipment. This equipment will have to include sound output (speakers or headsets) and microphones. It's not that either of these is a big deal or very expensive, but they are not standard equipment now and they will have to be.

Last, full VOIP integration will likely also call for a whole new area of IT expertise and infrastructure in your organization. Again, these are probably not insurmountable challenges, but certainly challenges that will have to be planned and provided for.

So, finding your voice in relation to web conferencing really comes down to three things: telephone audio conferencing, VOIP, or VOIP-like functionality over standard phone lines. In this chapter, we examine all three.

Telephone Audio Conferencing

Audio conference calls in conjunction with any kind of web conference can occur in a number of ways. In a small organization or at home, voice integration with a web meeting usually occurs when one person has three-way calling as a standard service on the phone line dials in two other parties. Of course, such meetings are therefore limited to three people, so if you have more than three participants, you need another way to manage the audio portion of your web conference.

Other ways require building and supporting an in-house audio conferencing system or contracting with a third-party audio conferencing provider. In a large organization, an in-house audio conferencing system is probably nothing more than a souped-up voice network that sports a Virtual Private Network or one or more Private Leased Lines. These will be unattended systems, which means that users have direct access to them with no operator assistance.

This system therefore will be based on an audio conferencing bridge to the organization's existing network node, typically called the PBX (Private Branch Exchange) and all calls will travel from the PBX to the bridge that connects the organization to the rest of the world. Think of the PBX as a main switchboard for the organization's telephone system. The organization's private voice network can connect all of its sites regardless of where in the world those sites are, and in order to speak to the rest of the planet, there are connections to the various PSTNs (public switched telephone networks) that allow the population of the world to speak to each other (see Figure 7.1).

This is all very cool stuff, even if we are all so used to it that we find it boring. Actually, we are lucky to be able to find it boring because it works so well. It's been working well for over thirty years and people

Figure 7.1. PBX, PSTN, and private voice network.

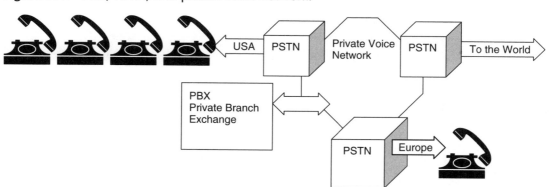

are very comfortable with it. Problem? It's expensive. Even though you own and are maintaining your own equipment, you have to pay for just about every type and minute of service you use beyond whatever your monthly stipend is to your telecommunications' services providers.

So, another way to incorporate audio into web conferencing is to use an outsourced audio conferencing solution in which all of your equipment, software, connections, operator assistance, and so on are provided, managed, and maintained by a third party. Depending on your use of voice conferencing as a stand-alone communications methodology or as an adjunct to web conferencing, this can be a more cost-effective solution than purchasing your own equipment. If you decide to go this way, you have a plethora of CSPs (conference service provider . . . because there just aren't enough acronyms in your life) to choose from. Two examples follow.

AT&T: Audio Conferencing CSP

Liz is old enough to remember when there really was just one phone company in the United States, and everyone called it Ma Bell. Anti-trust laws took care of that, and now we have lots of Baby Bells to contend with along with a few major competitors including the mono-liths of AT&T, Sprint, or MCI to name just a few. These companies all offer local service, long distance service, digital services, and satellite services. It's all quite overwhelming. It's even more overwhelming when you sit down and try to figure out the best way to construct your telecommunications life. It's a skill that even we have not yet mastered, but we're working on it.

The nice thing about using a CSP like AT&T for your voice confer-encing needs is that if you are also using them for other aspects of your phone service(s), you can probably get an integrated service and a single account to manage. The bad part is that you usually have to pay for all the little conveniences in this life, so you'll need to com-pare pricing for the services that you get.

If you choose a company like AT&T to outsource your audio con-ferencing, you will have a host of services and features you can choose from. AT&T Teleconferencing Services (at www.att.com) offer you some of the following:

- Toll-free conferences or caller-paid. In other words, you provide your participants with a toll-free number to dial into, or not. This is becoming surprisingly cost effective; there are a lot of small telecommunications companies out there that offer very affordable subscription rates for toll-free numbers. Customers like toll-free numbers for obvious reasons.

- Digital recording of teleconferences that you can distribute electronically to a voice mailbox or on audio cassette.

- A reservation-less system that allows you to call meetings on demand by using a preassigned dial-in number and access code that's always available to you.

- The ability to coordinate your audio conference with whatever web conferencing solution you've chosen. You'll not be surprised to know that AT&T has a web conferencing product, too, but whether you use it or another vendor's, you can still use AT&T for the audio portion.

- AT&T Conference Manager, which gives a call's host the ability to monitor and control audio conference calls via the Internet without the help of what's called at Teleconferencing Specialist— or what the rest of us still call an operator. The Conference Manager's features include:

  - Selection of broadcast mode (everyone can talk) or two-way interactive mode only (whereby the host and one other person can speak, everyone else can just listen until they're queued to speak)

  - Q&A Session Administration whereby the host is able to see who is requesting permission to ask a question, and can queue those requests as s/he desires

  - Control of exit and entry tones as people attend/leave the call

  - The ability to get operator assistance on the fly even if you've used a reservation-less access

- The ability to dial out by yourself and add someone to the call who perhaps didn't know about the conference when it started but whose input is now desired

- The ability to disconnect call participants as you see fit. A fun feature for all you power-hungry types out there

Running an Effective Audio Conference

- Before a call, make sure you've invited key participants and confirm they have the date, time, and call-in number.

- Encourage everyone to use a land line, not a cell or an airplane phone unless absolutely unavoidable.

- Provide all materials salient to the call to participants in advance.

- Start on time.

- Have everyone introduce themselves and review the call agenda.

- Ask everyone to identify themselves when they first begin to speak, and every time they speak.

- Encourage people to use their "mute" button when not speaking to cut down on background noise.

- End the conference on time and distribute minutes/action items promptly.

Biggest Not Necessarily Best: ACT Teleconferencing

AT&T is certainly not the only game in town for audio conferencing. You do have lots of choices. ACT Teleconferencing is such an example.

For the most part, ACT's audio conferencing capabilities mirror what you can get from AT&T, but they do have a couple of tricks up their sleeve as well in the form of three distinct types of audio conferencing services.

ReadyConnect Reservation-Less Conferencing

The first is called ReadyConnect, which is an automated conferencing service that mirrors the reservation-less system offered by AT&T. The second is called ActionCall, which is an attended conferencing service that does require reservations and that does offer operator assistance. The third is what they call Passcode with which access to audio conferencing is limited to select participants who you give a conference ID number or a passcode.

If you choose ReadyConnect, you can access it via a toll-free call. In the ACT lexicon, the hosts of these conferences are called chairpersons and each chairperson in your organization is issued a ReadyConnect calling card that features two PIN numbers, one for her and one for participants. It's also the calling card that will give the toll-free versus the toll call dial-in numbers. These numbers remain valid for every chairperson to whom you issue authority and a calling card.

ReadyConnect allows the chairperson to accurately identify the audience through an audible list of participants. Participants are asked to record their name when they enter the conference. It also features the ability to lock the conference once everyone who's supposed to be in there is in there, the ability for the chairperson to put the participants in listen-only mode as well as mute his own instrument, and the ability to record the conference. Last, as with AT&T, the chairperson has the ability to dial out to participants, but this is limited to calls in the United States.

ActionCall

With ActionCall, there's a choice of access methods. You can use:

- Local Meet Me Conferencing for which each participant dials a preassigned phone number and is immediately connected to the conference call. This enables participants to join a call from anywhere in the world using their own long distance provider.

- Toll-Free Meet Me Conferencing in which each participant dials a preassigned toll-free number and is immediately connected to the conference call.

- Dial-out Conferencing by which each participant is called at their own phone number by an ACT conference coordinator and is then connected to the conference. The idea here is that all conference bridging and long distance charges are billed to a single party. The service is intended to save time (because the initiative is being taken to get everyone connected as scheduled) and to also lend both a professional and personal touch to the conference.

Added features of ActionCall are:

- Full assistance from a conference coordinator assigned to the call who can be reached by pressing *0 at anytime. It should be noted that a coordinator is monitoring the conference all the time and that all ACT coordinators sign confidentiality agreements. If you don't want this monitoring, don't use ActionCall or specify that you want to make other arrangements.

- Standing reservations for regularly scheduled meetings up to and beyond one year in advance.

- Broadcast/Lecture mode, which is used to increase effectiveness on larger conference calls in which the presenter speaks to the participants who are all on listen-only mode from the get-go.

- Sub-conferencing, or the ability to meet confidentially with call participants or call speakers before and/or after the conference to prepare for or review the conference. A sub-conference can also be held at any time during a conference call for breakout group meetings.

- Transferring conferences by which an entire conference, a group from a conference, or just a single person can be transferred from one conference to another in progress.

- Participant recall feature that allows the call coordinator to automatically get someone back if they've been dropped for any reason.

In addition to these, ActionCall has some advanced features that mirror the sort of Q&A, polling, voting, recording, replaying, transcribing, and off-line chat features that are also commonplace to web conferencing these days.

So it's here where ACT Teleconferencing's name might again seem to be a misnomer. They are not just about teleconferencing, and even in their audio services they are dancing closer and closer to the sorts of things we think will be commonplace once VOIP takes over. ACT, like many in their space, are already starting to offer these kinds of hybrid functionalities. But before we get to the mixed breeds, let's take a good look at pure Voice Over IP.

VOIP—More than Just a Pretty Acronym

Voice Over Internet Protocol (VOIP) first appeared in the mid 1990s in the form of an Internet phone that allowed two people, anywhere in the world, to talk to one another using PCs equipped with video cameras, microphones, and Internet connections. It's still got a long way to go before it is as seamless, reliable, and boring to use as our regular phone service, but there are lots of reasons that its perfection is being pursued. And if the history of technology tells us anything, that perfection will be attained shortly because service providers and manufacturers anticipate that VOIP has great revenue potential.

VOIP allows people to use the same bandwidth for data and voice communications simultaneously. The resulting benefits include positive effects on network load balancing, lower long distance costs, and the ability to really do multimedia media in a single view. Frankly, this is nothing less than fully leveraging the capabilities of the Internet and lowering communications costs at the same time. That's huge! The pursuit of this by technologists everywhere is a no-brainer.

But there are, or at least there will be, other benefits to VOIP beyond pure cost savings and maximizing bandwidth use. Bandwidth, for those of you who haven't heard the term before, is the actual physical capacity of a cable or a wire to carry data, or voice, or whatever "stuff" is being transmitted. For example, VOIP communications will be as scalable as networks are now. For most organizations, this will mean just adding more ports to a VOIP gateway which is simpler, requires less hardware and wiring, and will be that much easier to maintain than adding ports and instruments to a VPN.

Using VOIP, voice transmissions are treated like data transmission. Data are much more malleable than voice. The data can be chopped up, edited, stored, and more. VOIP makes voice just as flexible so it can also be chopped up, edited, stored, and so on. In other words, voice data will be able to be transferred and manipulated in ways not possible now.

Perhaps most pertinent of all, when VOIP is ubiquitous the entire communications system of an organization will have a single design and a single interface to all users. We don't know that VOIP is going to replace the telephone, but it's going to give telephone networks a run for their money; some of the major players in VOIP tomorrow are guaranteed to be the major (and minor) players in telephone telecommunications today. In fact, according to the Eastern Management Group, sales of VOIP-based systems are beginning to outpace sales of PBX-based systems. In 2001 about 2,000 more VOIP-based systems were sold in the United States. The gap is expected to increase to 6,000 units annually in the next year or so. What will make this prediction true or false will be the performance of the technology. The longer it takes to make it pretty near perfect, the longer it will take for it to outsell the old-school technology. It might not happen as fast as the Eastern Management Group believes, but it will happen.

Forget for a second that Voice Over IP may, sooner than we think, save us physical space by replacing telephone and fax units in favor of a PC for all our telecom needs, including faxing and voicemail. VOIP is already better than traditional phone networks because it makes better use of existing bandwidth.

In an analog phone network, voice is transmitted at a frequency of 3.1 kHz. Even in ISDN, which stands for Integrated Services Digital Network, and which is a system of digital phone connections, only speeds of 8kHZ or 64kbps are available for telephony. Now a telephone connection has sufficient quality at 5.3 to 6.4kbps, so the rest of the bandwidth used to carry standard phone transmissions is wasted space.[1]

OK? Still with us? Have a headache? Hang in there . . . we're almost done and you'll be happy to have a clue about all this.

VOIP, by transmitting voice over the same lines used for data, enables several voice connections on one line. This is called multiplexing, and it means that bandwidth is being used more efficiently; therefore, transmissions are occurring faster. By extension, transmissions are also occurring cheaper.

VOIP: Not Quite Ready for Primetime

To write this book, we actually ran, were walked through, or took advantage of the self-paced demo tours that exist for each of the products we chose to feature.

Most of the VOIP vendors offer audio conferencing services and can coordinate them with your VOIP products and services. However, Interwise was the only vendor brave enough to run our demo using their VOIP technology. It was not perfect, but it was good. The setup was moderately difficult and not particularly intuitive, though Liz was able to manage it without Sue.

Interestingly during the demo, even with a high-powered system with sufficient bandwidth and speed for data, voice, and video conferencing we experienced buffer delays or intermediate memory requirements. These delays significantly chopped up the flow of the conversation with Jennifer Chisholm, VP of Marketing for Interwise who ran the demo of the product. A buffer, in a lay definition, is a space in which any datum, in this case, our voices, is sent and then relayed to wherever it's supposed to go after it's been digitized and converted between the packet-driven system and the line-relaying system.* So in the case of VOIP from Interwise, the buffer would get full before all of what Jennifer was saying would reach Liz' speakers, and there would be about ten seconds of silence while it caught up. Annoying yes, but just a delay in transmission. None of what Jennifer

---

*Data on the Internet are typically transmitted in groupings called packets. Voice transmissions typically occur over line-relaying systems. Since VOIP is voice data being transmitted to PCs that may be getting the data via land phone lines, these translations are necessary.

was saying was ever completely lost. However, had it not been a fairly laid-back demonstration but rather an important sales presentation or PR announcement, it would have been distracting enough to affect people's perception of the quality of the encounter.

We don't mention this as a knock on Interwise; as we said, they were the only ones with strong enough capabilities in VOIP to even try it with us knowing we would write about it. We simply point it out as an example of what will need to happen for VOIP to become as commonplace as—or take the place of—the telephone.

Eventually VOIP will have consequences for all businesses that use the telephone (so that would pretty much be everybody) that go beyond even its coordination with web conferencing. Although beyond the scope of this book, it would be irresponsible of us not to at least mention these things because you are going to be hearing about them, and as you begin to use VOIP more (and you will), you will need to know about them. These consequences can be grouped under the umbrella name of Unified Messaging.

In short, unified messaging happens when all communications, voice, data, fax, email, interactive voice response, voice mail, call centers, automatic call distribution, you name it, is transmitted over the Internet from a single server. It might not make the telephone obsolete, but it will likely make the kind of third-party telecommunications companies that maintain and support equipment for audio conferencing obsolete. And certainly it will force them to "upgrade" from being telecommunications vendors to ISPs (Internet services providers).

For Now, Mix and Match

An option that exists in this netherworld between pure audio conferencing and exclusive use of VOIP is to use a hybrid solution where you are not really using a third party to secure and maintain the equipment you need to support your audio conferencing needs, but you are using a third party to provide the functionality of web-like communications over your PC network and/or your phone network.

For example, you could consider partnering with a company like Genesys Conferencing Inc., which offers a highly redundant global bridge network that is able to absorb vast amounts of voice and data traffic over vast amounts of physical space via a sophisticated bridging system they built and maintain. A system that is redundant, by the way, is one that has backups and work-arounds and alternatives built into its scheme that are able to go around a problem point in a transmission rather than having to wait for it to clear. You can access Genesys' products and services either through standard telephony or via your Internet protocol, which is what makes it a hybrid solution.

Another alternative is something like MeetingPlace from Latitude which positions its conformity to strict Internet standards as its primary strength in the battle to achieve VOIP perfection and dominance because its products can be tightly integrated with other enterprise-wide telephony solutions.* In other words, the product is built to fit specifically into the space that exists between—or connects—the IP world to the PSTN world (see Figure 7.2).

And just to raise the bar a bit more, Latitude also expanded its IP communications integration and delivery capacities beyond voice to encompass multi-point video. What that means, boys and girls, is that not only will you be able to talk to others on your PC during a web conference, but you'll be able to see more than one other participant in the conference, and everybody will be able to speak and be heard depending upon the rights and queuing set up by the conference host.

As a third sort of alternative Voyant Technologies has products called ReadiVoice and ReadiVoice IP. ReadiVoice is designed to support more than 9,600 ports in a single application of telephony in order to provide single-source and fully integrated web conferencing data, voice, and multi-point video.

The ways in which ReadiVoice is differentiated from your mom's expandable PBX are things like its ability to always route connections

*Adherence to standards matters in Internet Protocol and Telephony technology, especially when the concern is lowering costs and maximizing the use of existing equipment.

Figure 7.2. IP/PSTN Connectivity.

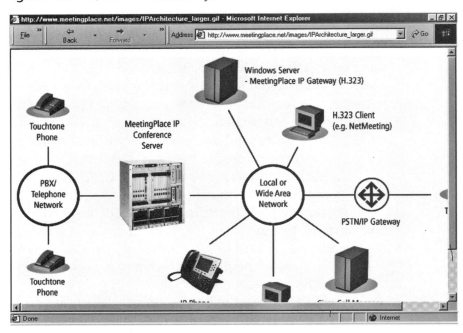

to servers and ports that are less crowded; or the fact that it supports SNMP (Simple Network Management Protocol, which does exactly what it sounds like it does: provides a simple protocol to manage your network); or its subscriber-driven ability to start, control, and view the dynamics of a conference via an IP phone (a bit more sophisticated than the picture phones introduced at the 1964 World's Fair, but it looks a little like that . . . or like your cell phone or PDA) or a PC. These are not features available to the standard phone system, especially since a phone that is not an IP phone offers no ability to view an image.

In short, the idea behind ReadiVoice IP is that it will allow the migration of an existing conferencing scheme to a packet-based scheme, which is more efficient and is faster and which will, eventually, better leverage the infrastructure of most organizations doing any sort of business or operations via Internet protocol which, again, will be just about the whole planet.

Interestingly, all of the vendors and products that we explored to bring this chapter to you sooner or later described their products as being intuitive. To be intuitive is to be able to know something by instinct and without reasoning, to have sharp insights. It's a good word to describe the reality that is taking over telephony. All of our voice systems are moving to a capability by which they will just have to be there, instantly coordinated with whatever else we are doing. This is evidenced not only in the pursuit of perfection for voice over Internet protocol, but in most of our daily lives, right now, by the sheer complexity, range of service, scope of features, and yet ease of use represented by the digital cell phones we already own.

It may never come to artificial intelligence or our PCs calling us at the ball game when a circuit blows in the house or the puppy is ripping up the furniture, but then, it just might. It will, however, most certainly come to a fully integrated desktop for web, voice, video, data, pictures, you name it. It's already here . . . it's just not boring yet.

Note

1. Torsten Schulz. Voice over IP, white paper, Eicon Technology Corporation (February, 2000), www.conferzone.com.

Using Web Conferencing to Deliver Your Content

Today the primary uses of web conferencing are for real-time meetings, broadcast announcements to large audiences in different locations, and outward bound sales and marketing presentations. There are two big reasons for this. First, there are many excellent prepackaged products for these applications, and second, people are just beginning to get comfortable with this technology. But as this technology explodes into more common use, one of its primary values will be found in employee training and development.

The vendors in this chapter have a particular focus on web conferencing as it applies to training and development. So you have the web conferencing functions combined with the ability to create and deliver course content. To illustrate what is available for delivering courseware over web conferencing, we've chosen Centra Software Inc., WorkWorlds Human Resources Corporation, and MindLeaders. Please note that there are only about a gazillion e-learning providers out there in the world. If you don't believe us, do your own Google search on "content providers" and see what you get.

We chose these three because they are great examples of the three ways to use web conferencing to deliver training: live e-learning with programs that your own organization has developed; instructor-led, typically live, programs that are provided by a third party; and prerecorded, prepackaged training programs that you can select from a catalog. These three methods are represented in turn by Centra, WorkWorlds, and MindLeaders.

But First, Some Dollars and Sense

In chapter three examining the business case, we looked at the hard numbers that dictate whether or not web conferencing for meetings, broadcasts, training, and so on support the argument that there is a cost saving associated with using web conferencing. All indications are that in terms of hard dollar expenditures, such as travel to name one, web conferencing can and does represent a positive return on investment. But the question when applied to e-learning mechanisms requires that you measure the value of the training by linking the training solution you choose to the business goals of the organization.[1]

Connecting the training to the business goals to determine the value of the e-learning is tied first and foremost to doing a serious analysis of what those goals are and how best to select/structure training that supports them. This may be a part of the assessment exercise performed when first looking for web conferencing technology, but it may not. Even if your organization has already adopted the technology for the more classic meeting/announcement needs of the organization, you should still do an in-depth analysis relative to business goals before you launch your web conferencing training applications.

Like all soft benefits, savings relative to them are hard to measure. These soft benefits are such things as increased productivity due to training efforts, employee retention, job satisfaction, and the like.[2] One way to measure savings is via comparison of results between classroom trained personnel versus e-learning trained personnel in the performance of a given skill. In other words, train a group of employees the old-fashioned way and train another group the new-fangled way and then compare their performance at the task either by written or practical exam.

Another way is to take the same group of employees, train them to do the same thing using both methods about a week apart, and then apply an evaluation tool to determine which they liked more and felt was more productive and ultimately satisfying.

Another interesting example of measuring the soft benefit of e-learning comes to us from the U.S. Army's Battle Command Training Program (BCTP).[3] The BCTP conducts battle training for the National Guard. They created e-learning preparation courses that guardsmen can use prior to going to the brick and mortar training. Among other uses the Army gets from this model is that they are able to measure the effectiveness of the live, in-person training for those who have had exposure to e-learning prior to coming to the course(s) versus those who have not. This is a blended learning solution that involves a combination of live workshops and e-learning.

More Documentation About the Value of Training Is Available

According to an Industry Report on the Business Case for Training that was released by the American Society of Trainers & Developers (ASTD) in January 2003, training investments are holding their value, and a larger portion of training budgets are going to e-learning initiatives.[4]

ASTD reported that despite the downturn in the economy after September 11, 2001, there was no downturn in total training expenditures by the organizations that participate in their benchmarking service. Further, these organizations continue to tout the importance of employee training and development in maintaining competitive advantage, contributing to growth and creativity and for long-term success.

Between 2000 and 2001, the percentage of training delivered by e-learning increased from 8.8 percent of total training hours to 10.5 percent of total training hours. This increase was the largest ever reported by ASTD in four years of looking at e-learning strategies.

E-learning is an idea whose time has come. In order to come along with it, you need to know what your options are for delivering training content over the Net. Your primary options follow.

Centra Symposium: Specializing in Curriculum Development Tools

In a nutshell, Symposium is a virtual classroom application; it is a method of delivering training to large or small groups of dispersed people that replicates typical classroom interaction in real time over intranets, extranets, or the Internet. And although other products, including some that we've looked at such as WebEx's or Interwise's training solutions, have some of the same features and functionalities of Symposium, this product goes that extra mile philosophically in terms of specifically supporting content development for training.

This support is provided by what Centra calls their Content Composition and Management Interface. It's a product that's capable of doing a lot. This makes it both valuable once you've learned all its parts, and confusing until you do. Not to worry—we're here to help ease the confusion.

Symposium's Content Composition and Management Interface consists of three functions: a content management application, a course cataloging product, and a set of authoring. Each of these are designed to work either in cooperation with or independently of one another. So there's quite a bit for us to break down and explain in order to empower you to use these tools well.

Before we get to that, we'll take a look at some of the elements of the Symposium product.

The first thing you'll notice about Symposium's various interfaces is that all of them have a Windows, Internet Explorer, Outlook (or sometimes all three) look and feel about them that most people will recognize. Figure 8.1 shows Knowledge Center, Symposium's content management application. You can see that the page has a familiar feel. That's a good thing too; if they had tried to create their own look and feel for things on top of all of the content support Symposium delivers, it may have been too much for the average bear to, well, bear.

Here are some of the functions of Symposium's content delivery strategy that will feel familiar to those who are or have used web conferencing technology for meetings or broadcasts:

- Synchronous learning tools such a online breakout rooms and labs

- Evaluation and assessment tools

Figure 8.1. Knowledge Center.

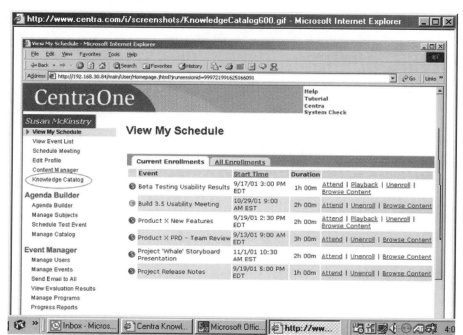

- Real-time feedback tools, such as laughter, applause, pacing, and comprehension, called emoticons—the ability to add some emotion to the comments and interactions between and among class participants

The product also sports a pretty good integrated VOIP. Symposium supports multi-point video conferencing, application sharing in real time, private and public chats, WebSafari or the ability of the instructor to take everyone to other websites, and the ability to annotate PowerPoint and whiteboard content.

Multi-point video means that more than one image can be seen at a time. In other words, if the instructor and four participants have PC cameras, their images, or whatever they'd like to put on camera, can be seen at any one time. However, only one of these images can be "streamed," which means that only one will have any animation with it. The others will be seen as still images.

There also support for multiple presenters, as well as the ability for participants to leave the class and put up an icon that indicates they are doing so. Not all of what can occur in Symposium has to occur live. There are asynchronous delivery tools, too, including the following:

- Support for recording, indexing, and editing
- Live and self-paced (previously recorded) blended content
- Self-paced content viewing, which enables the organization to configure sessions to allow enrolled participants access to content before and after the live session

So to summarize, Symposium in its physical design looks, feels, and operates pretty much the same way as the other web conferencing product you've read about in this book. This is not a bad thing because familiarity with the dynamics of all of these products is what will ultimately gain their wider adoption and use. But Symposium is differentiated from other products by the functions that support content design and content development Let's look at those now.

Content Management

The major component of Symposium's product is Knowledge Center, the content management application. This application does exactly what the name implies: It provides tools to manage the training content you design. It is made up of three main parts: personalized learning capabilities, knowledge object authoring tools, and learning content management tools.

Personalized learning capabilities allow you to do the following:

- Tie specific knowledge objects* to individual training needs. This means that the content you design for training can be tied to the requirements for training that any individual or job function in your organization has.

- Access information and learning activities that are indexed by job function, title, type, and category. This allows you to categorize the training so that the right information and exercises are made available to people who do jobs in your organization that require that type of training.

- Support blended, self-paced learning. This means that some of the training your people get can be live, some of it prerecorded, and all of it accessible in a way that they access at their own speed.

- Track an individual's current and previous skill levels. This helps people determine how they're doing with their learning curve.

The Knowledge Object Authoring tools are made possible by the Knowledge Composers, which allow any user to quickly create and publish editable, standards-compliant content** using familiar applications like PowerPoint. On top of that, the Object Authoring tools also support wizards and templates that allow for quick creation or import

---

*A "knowledge object," sometimes called a "content object" or a "learning object," is what we older folks used to just call "information."

**Content that meets the standards for presentation in your organization or content that meets industry standards for whatever it is you are training on.

of assessments, URL reference, surveys, multiple choice questions, and FAQs. Learning Content Management refers to the ability to manage both your own custom-created as well as that from third-party sources. In order to be able to easily find third-party content you might be interested in using, Symposium has an indexing tool that can search for and retrieve content over the Internet by name, category, and type.

In short, Symposium's Knowledge Center is the repository for all content related to training or e-learning and the place where users can access it. Further, it also has all of the actual content creation tools you'll need to create the content in the first place. It has a lot of horsepower, but is only as robust as you need it to be. You can choose to stick with easy-to-create and easy-to-manipulate presentation tools like PowerPoint or import content from websites. That will be fine; the product will support your increasing creativity as you gain the confidence to explore everything it has to offer.

Cataloging Your Training Content

The Knowledge Catalog, the second part of the Content Composition scheme, organizes all of the content created and maintained by an individual or organization so it is easy to search, retrieve, deliver, and track. It is a self-service library of recorded content (see Figure 8.2).

But beyond simply being a catalog where you can go look things up and pick and choose, the Knowledge Catalog can also be used to recommend pre- and post-work for a given session. So participants can be prompted to look at a specific set of documents before their course begins, or be directed to post-work to reinforce the learning points of a training session.

So right here, in just these two examples of Knowledge Center and Knowledge Catalog, you can see that there is another level of ingenuity that is being applied by content support and design providers such as Centra that goes beyond web conferencing products that have a "space" for training. If content design and maintenance is your cup of tea, these products can surely help.

Using Web Conferencing to Deliver Your Content

117

Figure 8.2. Knowledge Catalog.

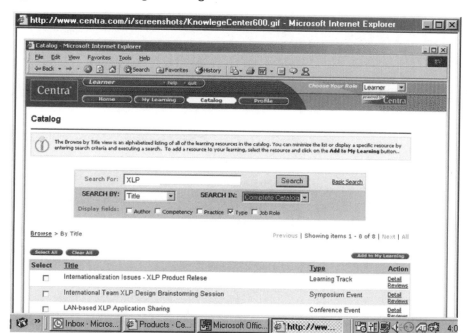

Creating Your Own Content

Symposiums Composers are the specific authoring tools for component-based authoring. Instructional designers can create, assemble, and organize information in order to develop a training program. These elements can be anything you can think of: text, graphics, audio, video, animations, simulations, or html files.

The Composer tools actually number three: the Pro package, the Composer for PowerPoint, and the Composer for Simulations. All three are optional, which means you don't have to use them in order to use Symposium's other features. But if you do choose to use them, they integrate seamlessly with the Knowledge Center. And all three can be used independently or in any combination with the others.

Figure 8.3. Symposium's Composer.

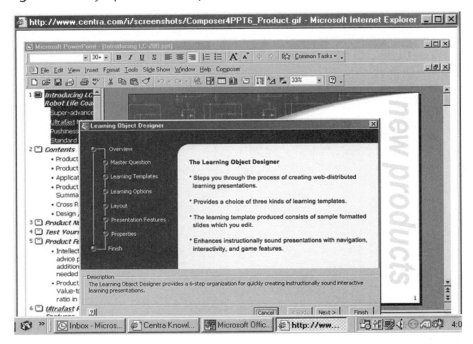

Composer Pro provides the following functions:

- Creates and stores learning objects in a single place in the Knowledge Center.

- Provides preconfigured templates for all sorts of information that you might want to include in your course. For example, let's say you wanted to use a table or a pie chart to illustrate some information. You'll find table and pie chart templates in Composer that you can simply plug your data into.

- Rich media support allows you to to combine text, graphics, audio, video, animation, assessment items, and html content to create some really funky and interesting courseware.

PowerPoint-specific use of Composer technology really is appropriate for presentations that need to be updated frequently or rapidly,

Figure 8.4. Symposium Delivery Mechanisms.

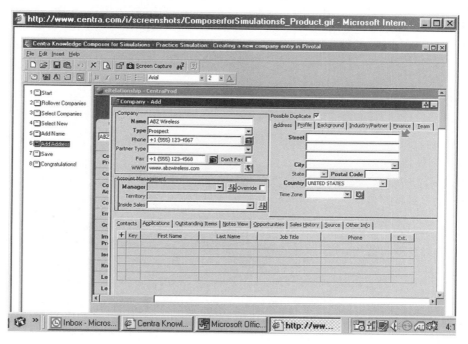

like product information or orientation materials. Subject matter experts and business professionals can create interactive, web-ready content using PowerPoint templates that are all set up to work with Symposium's delivery mechanisms (see Figure 8.3).

Simulations are used to demonstrate the operation of something in your training session (see Figure 8.4). In other words, let's say that BizMarked is putting together a training course about a router they support from the Acme Router Company. A demonstration of how the router is installed in a server could be plugged into the training course using Symposium's simulation tool. This tool consists of pre-configured templates for creating and publishing interactive software (the key word here of course being "interactive") that will work well in demonstration and product process presentation and courses. Again, these templates are designed to seamlessly integrate with the delivery mechanisms of Symposium.

We hope that the last pages will increase, or have increased, your comfort level with using tools like Symposium to streamline and maximize your content development, maintenance, and delivery. If doing one, two, or all three of these things is part of your job description, then you should know there is excellent software out in the world to help you. Hopefully now you won't be overwhelmed when you visit a site like Centra's and are bombarded by what the product can do.

Now, let's turn our attention to instructor-led program providers.

WorkWorlds: Leading by Instructors

As with most sites that have anything to do with web conferencing, a visit to WorkWorlds can be overwhelming until you take a deep breath and examine the organization of their site and their services. We chose them because, while they can boast of a "whole lotta shakin' goin' on," their site is well segmented and easy to navigate after a few minutes of surfing it. Most important to our purpose here, Work-Worlds has an extremely well-diversified set of offerings in instructor-led programming.

First of all, the correct semantics for the types of programs that WorkWorlds offers is seminars. WorkWorld's founder Beth I. Warren, who is the might behind this machine, would be very upset with us if we didn't get that right from the get go.

WorkWorlds positions its eSeminars as being state-of-the-art products of its E-Institute that provide a full spectrum of educational programs for diverse organizations and individuals of the global village. With its exemplar faculty and technologically robust WebBased Conference Center, powered by WebEx, the E-Institute learning experiences are being positioned to strategically surpass those of the traditional classroom. WorkWorlds' philosophy is borrowed from Eric Hoffer who said, "In times of change, learners inherit the earth, while the learned find themselves equipped to deal with a world that no longer exists." Deep, but true. If Liz were to rephrase this for the 21st century reader, she'd say it was: "Lead, follow, or get run over."

Notice that WorkWorlds offers its programs using WebEx; in fact as of this writing, they use WebEx meeting center functionality as opposed to WebEx training. This may change, and given the fine-tuning of its Training Center that WebEx is currently engaging in, we wouldn't be a bit surprised if WorkWorlds changes over to the WebEx Training Center as the eSeminar delivery mechanism soon.

e-Seminar Features

The first thing that differentiates WorkWorlds from Symposium or from MindLeaders, as we'll see in a few pages, is that WorkWorlds' content development and delivery is dependent upon real people, real professional instructors in fact, doing real curriculum design and real teaching. Amazing. The qualities offered by such a model are content expertise, adjunct faculty who have a deep understanding of the underpinnings of adult learning, and professionals who are mentors for seminar attendees. There are things you just can't get from software, no matter how sophisticated it is, and these are things that allow for a high degree of customization of the information.

Our View   *Here's an example: Liz, as we told you at the beginning of this book, is an educational consultant with a targeted expertise in diversity. She actually has Beth Warren of WorkWorlds to thank (or blame) for bringing the wide world of instructor-led eSeminars to her attention because they "met" (as with so many relationships on this cyber-planet these days, they've never actually met) when Beth sent out a mail blast inviting people to an eSeminar and Liz responded by saying that not only might she like to attend the seminar, but she thought she could teach some too. Big mouth.*

One thing led to another, one of those being this book, and Liz did develop a program about diversity in the workplace for WorkWorlds. Liz' programs are typically scheduled to run on a given day/time. WorkWorlds instructors have the option of booking days/times as many months in advance if they'd like. If enrollment justifies the class taking place, then invitations are sent out to the enrollees giving them the URL and password for the eSeminar on the day and at the time they enrolled for, and away we all go.

On one occasion, Beth came upon an opportunity to have Liz do her eSeminar for a group of people who were all journalists or who worked for media companies. Because Liz knew in advance that this would be the construct of the attendees for that particular session, she was able to customize her content to meet their needs. Examples, statistics, and case studies from that market sector were used, as opposed to had all of the attendees been dialing in, say, from Wall Street in which case the same kinds of data would have been drawn from Liz' experience working in the financial industry. The ability to customize instructor-led classes is definitely one of its huge advantages over using prepackaged programs, but of course, it's also more work for the instructor.

Seek and Ye Shall Find

As you observe from the picture in Figure 8.5, potential participants can search the WorkWorlds' catalog of eSeminars by category or by instructor. If you choose to look by instructor and you select Beth

Figure 8.5. WorkWorlds' eSeminar Search Page.

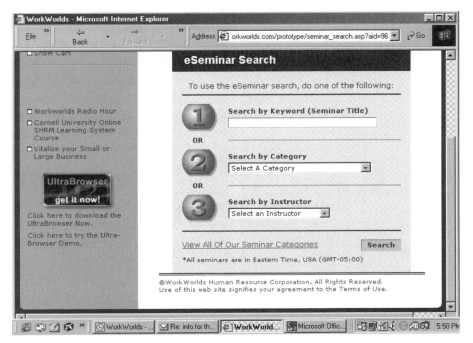

Warren, for example, from the pull-down menu, you'll see something like the display in Figure 8.6.

Here we see that the top of the page lists the various eSeminars that Beth teaches, a brief description, when they're next scheduled to be offered, and what categories of HR or OD they are applicable to. You can also get more details about a seminar and more details about Beth her own livin' self.

If you examine the categories for a moment, you'll see that they are very eclectic. You can search for courses by category in the initial search screen, or you can click on any of them from a particular instructor's profile to see what WorkWorlds has up its sleeve in HR issues, those strategic people issues of the workplace (see Figure 8.7).

So, if you click on Human Resources, you'll see information as represented in Figure 8.6. Naturally there'd be a lot more of it than what's represented in this example, but hopefully you get the idea.

Figure 8.6.   WorkWorlds' Results Page.

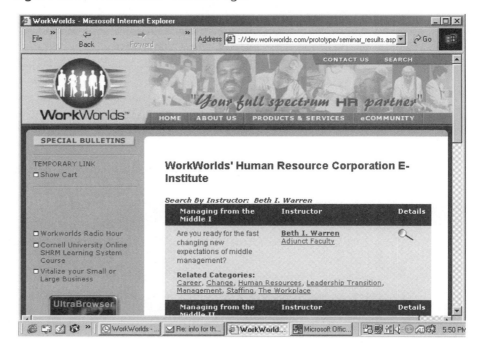

Figure 8.7.   Sample of WorkWorlds' Categories.

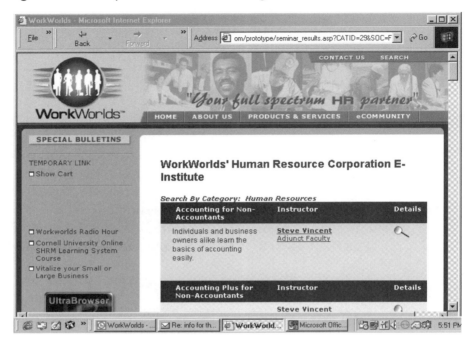

A Great Deal to Offer

The range and breath of the offerings of organizations like Work-Worlds is practically limitless.

In terms of professional development, WorkWorlds and similar vendors offer professional development courses in a range of disciplines including (but not limited to certainly) professional certification for PHRs (Professional in Human Resources) and SPHRs (Senior Professional in Human Resources). There are eSeminars that are offered in conjunction with professional organizations—everyone from HR to accountants to legal specialties, and everything in between. Since we're using WorkWorlds as an example of all this, they have a relationship with Cornell to offer professional development eSeminars for SPHRs or PHRs.

There's a lot to learn in this wide world of ours—sometimes a good teacher makes all the difference.

MindLeaders: Build It and They Will Enroll

And then there are times that even a good teacher will get in the way of a person trying to learn something. For times like those, there's a third option for training via web conferencing: predesigned, prepackaged training. An organization that excels in this is called MindLeaders.

MindLeaders used to be called DPEC Inc., and they've been around since 1981. This is interesting to us because there really wasn't an Internet to speak of that was familiar to anyone but techie diehards in government (read: military and defense), academia, and high tech (consisting of the sort of folks who found—and still find—it hard to talk to the rest of us) back in 1981. So we surmise that Carol Clark who founded and is president of DPEC/MindLeaders started out delivering her wares on floppy disks, and probably the sort of floppy that resembled a 45 rpm record. We're not sure that any of this history matters except that it certainly speaks to MindLeaders' experience in knowing how to deliver prepackaged training content to adults in the workplace regardless of the medium used to deliver it.

MindLeaders, like the other providers in the prepackaged training space, is focused on two things: quality of product and effective pricing for the product. They offer over 800 courses (no, we won't be listing them) specifically developed (these days) in native HTML (Hyper Text Markup Language, the language that webpages are written in) to enable real-time presentations via the Internet. "Real time" in Mind-Leaders' world refers to the fact that, even though the courses can be downloaded by individuals and taken at the individual's pace, they can also be downloaded by an instructor taking a group of remote users through the course at the same time. As with Symposium and WorkWorlds, have browser, can learn, applies here too.

The pricing is subscription based so it eliminates the need for an organization to guess in advance what courses its employees are going to want or need. Once the organization has paid its subscription for a group of courses, its members with authorization can access those courses as many times as they need to.

To help make their offerings easy to access, MindLeaders has established partnerships with over 1,300 ISPs (Internet service providers) and 125 other marketing partners in order to ensure that the ISPs can accommodate any and all of the formats or templates that the MindLeaders courseware uses. Their website provides a list of these ISPs and partners. To help ensure quality of their course offerings, MindLeaders is a member of the Microsoft Independent Courseware Vendor (ICV) program and must therefore adhere to strict course-development standards.

Of course it's hard to say if being a member of the Microsoft ICV ensures quality. On the one hand, it's hard to argue with an entity that has basically taken over the world in less than fifteen years; on the other hand, one man's quality is another man's garbage. We will say though that adherence to such standards will make all of the Mind-Leaders courses have a similar look and feel for users and many people take comfort in that. In fact, MindLeaders positions its courses as being more desirable than instructor-led programs because consistency is built in. It's a valid point, but here we'd also throw up for consideration that one man's consistency is another man's boredom.

Not to beat this consistency point to death, but it does enable another feature that you'll find if you visit MindLeaders' site. That is the ability to demo a course. Since all the courses look and interact exactly the same, this is one instance where a demonstration is particularly valuable for prospective customers.

Still, one thing that prepackaged learning has going for it is that it is entirely self-paced; the user determines how far and how fast to go through a program. For anyone who's ever been frustrated by the pace of a class as being too fast or too slow, this is a tremendous selling point. And the self-paced nature of the prepackaged model also means that people can access it when they're ready, when they're available, or (if it was one of us) when they're trying to avoid doing something else.

Can't Tell the Players . . .

Eight hundred some odd course offerings is impressive, though potentially confusing. So MindLeaders breaks its online catalog into what they call Course Groups of which there are three: End User Grouping, Technical Grouping, and Insurance Professional Development.

End User Grouping consists of:

- Business skills development courses (think "time management" and the like)
- Desktop computing
- Home and small business (think how to use Quicken without attacking the accountant)

The Technical Grouping consists of courses dealing with topics in:

- General technology
- Mainframe technology
- Microsoft certifications (manifest destiny at play again)
- Web development

And the development courses for licensed insurance professionals are:

- The Insurance Professionals Exam Prep Course
- Introduction to Retirement
- Choosing a Qualified Plan
- Matching Plans With Clients, Funding and Administration
- Monetary Needs After Retirement
- Nonqualified Plans and Distribution

We expect MindLeaders to develop other professional development groupings over time. It certainly seems like growth area to us.

Features and Benefits

We chose MindLeaders to represent this space because, while they are not the only self-paced, prepackaged training provider, they do offer a lot. Consider what's possible if you decide to implement these programs.

- Skills assessment tools. These enable participants to determine their knowledge level, strengths/weaknesses relative to a given course or topic. And of course, there are post-tests. What would life be without tests?

- Pop-up questions. The questions come up at unspecified times in a variety of formats (fill in, multiple choice, T/F), and there is instant feedback as to whether the answer given is right or wrong. This sort of tool not only challenges the participant and should help to keep her engaged, but it also is another way of letting her know how she's doing with the coursework.

- Simulations. There is a plug-in (Macromedia Authorware Web Player) that enables the student to run simulations found in some—not all—MindLeaders courses.

- Exercises. Real-Life scenarios and case studies allow for skills to be practiced. What would life be without homework?

- Search capabilities. These enable the user to research any topic of interest within a course.

- Global bookmarking. This is the new age answer to the question, "Now, where was I?" Participants can bookmark their place in a course should they have to interrupt their studies. They can also bookmark places in the course that are of particular interest to them that they might want to come back to.

Beyond these features and benefits, MindLeaders is also cognizant of the fact that sometimes, you just need someone to talk to. Although they offer an Instant Mentoring service, which is like an "Ask Jeeves"* for this sort of application, it really constitutes only reinforcement of ideas or work the individual has already performed and is looking for feedback on. It really doesn't offer encouragement or direction; true education is seldom possible without both of those.

So within the MindLeaders model, you will find strong support for leveraging their offerings with blended learning whereby MindLead-

---

*www.askjeeves.com is a website on which you can ask question concerning just about any subject.

ers programs, for example, can be used as "pre-tests" to help determine what needs are before a third-party, instructor-led solution from a WorkWorld is chosen or a course is developed in-house using a product like Symposium.

They also stand up and cheer for using e-learning to serve as the method to gain initial skills in a discipline, as a reference tool for instructors, as a practical application or demonstration tool within an instructor-led course, or as a post-test mechanism to see how people really fared in the instructor-led course.

Summary

So as is true with most of life, there is more than one way to skin this training cat (with apologies to our own cats whom we would never skin). What's required, of course, as with all aspects of web conferencing adoption in your organization or in your life, is a complete understanding of what the needs are and what the culture will best support. If your organization—and your life—are like most, your needs are eclectic and your culture diverse. Blending the capabilities of all three models for education/training content development, maintenance, and delivery might be the ticket.

Notes

1. Sarah Fister Gale, "Measuring the ROI of E-Learning," *Workforce Magazine* (August 2002), pp. 74–77.
2. Ibid.
3. John S McCright, "E-Learning Scales Up—Huge Federal Training Programs Mix Net-Based Systems, Classroom Study," *eWeek* (August 5, 2002).
4. *Training for the Next Economy: An ASTD State of the Industry Report, ASTD* (January 2003), www.astd.org.

All About
Meetings

Chapter
9

After having looked at web conferencing generalists, project management specialists, and content delivery strategists, the only thing left to do is look at the vendors who specialize in the specific function of web conferencing that the technology really sprung up from: meetings.

In preceding chapters, especially in Chapter 5, which looked at the big picture, meeting capabilities certainly came up. But our research into all this told us that there are two things that shouldn't ever be given short shrift in some products. These are targeted and focused features of a web conferencing product for meetings with a reasonably sized group of people—say twenty or less—and products that take the needs of smaller organizations into consideration. By this we mean what these smaller firms have less in the way of resources to support their use of web conferencing. So a product they can use well has to take these modest resources into account.

If you are a small business that employs more than a dozen or so people, but less than 500, or if you think that your use of web conferencing will be strictly limited to (in the foreseeable future) running collaborative meetings among people in diverse locations in the United States and Canada, then you should consider the special features and functionalities of the following products. Again, we don't mean to imply in any way that any of these products—Placeware, Intercall, or Linktivity—aren't good for big companies. But they all tell a good story when your focus is meetings and your size is on the small side.

Just as we were putting the finishing touches on this book, we read that Microsoft had entered into an agreement to acquire PlaceWare. In part their joint press release said:

> Microsoft Corp. announced it has entered into an agreement to acquire PlaceWare Inc. to conduct real-time, interactive presentations and meetings over the Internet. By combining key assets and working in tandem, the two companies aim to provide customers with innovative and easy-to-use online conferencing solutions that will help connect more people seamlessly in a real-time conferencing environment. Microsoft also hopes to provide industry partners with improved technologies they can use to develop and deliver new custom business solutions that take advantage of advanced real-time collaboration capabilities. "This acquisition complements our business and is an important step forward in our strategy to expand our information worker solutions base," said Jeff Raikes, group vice president of Productivity and Business Services at Microsoft. "We look forward to merging our strengths to effectively deliver new real-time collaboration capabilities and solutions for this emerging and expanding online conferencing market." Microsoft also today announced the creation of a new business unit, the Real Time Collaboration Group, within the information worker business. With new Real Time Collaboration Group, Microsoft hopes to expand its current Web conferencing base to offer its customers and partners complete online business communication tools and solutions. The group plans to bring together Microsoft's various collaboration initiatives to more quickly and efficiently provide information workers with the tools and technologies they need to be more productive in and out of the office (February 2003).

Before this acquisition, Microsoft's product offerings specific to real-time collaboration among anyone using their operating system was limited to NetMeeting. NetMeeting is discussed in detail in Chapter 12 about transporting web conferencing collaboration tools and strategies to home use because it is much more limited in its features and abilities when compared to just about any other web conferencing product you might investigate. The point is, it was—and is—fine for home use, but its limitations make it a liability for the types of workplace collaboration we've been discussing to this point. Microsoft obviously agreed, and so went out and acquired Placeware so that it would be well positioned to participate in the exploding use of web conferencing for business collaboration and communications.

Setting a PlaceWare at the Table

PlaceWare's web conferencing solution for meetings has two main parts: Auditorium Places which is designed, as its name implies, for hosting large-scale structured events and conferences, and Web Meeting Places which is designed to replicate highly collaborative work environments found in focused small meetings. It is the Web Meeting Places' functionality that we'll concern ourselves with.

Web Meeting Places has all of the standard web conferencing features such as collaborative annotation tools, application and desktop sharing, private chat capabilities, and the like, but within these commonplace offerings are a few nuggets that are really boons for running small meetings.

First of these is in application sharing. A user can share a view of an application with all the other participants or they can share control of an application with another user. The person to whom sharing capabilities are being offered can control whether or not they are seeing the application as a full view or as a window within the full-screen interface. That means that they can be looking at a variety of things at the same time and can control which one, or ones, they want to pay particular attention to.

Another feature of the product great for small groups is the way that it allows opportunities for whiteboarding, web touring, or polls to be inserted into a set of PowerPoint slides that the host may be using to keep the meeting moving along. What this means is that the host can keep all of the elements of a meeting in one place so that she doesn't have to keep a whole set of windows open to go and grab things when it's time to. Nor does she have to keep notes to tell her that it is time to go to another view or application because that view or application will already be inserted into the flow of her presentation. This is really just a nice organizing feature of the product for small group collaborations where it's more likely that people are going to want to break down what they are talking about on the whiteboard or perhaps go surf the Net for some other information to augment the topic at hand.

PlaceWare does have a limited story for audio, but it is one-way streaming audio. This is different from VOIP because VOIP by definition can accommodate two-way communication. They also offer integrated teleconferencing with Web Meeting Places, but it really just amounts to using the telephone to connect all meeting participants with no systemic integration features between what's occurring on screen and what's being said.

Interestingly, there is no support for video, even single point video, in this product, but we don't think of that as a problem in this small meeting use of web conferencing software. Frankly, until video is able to support multi-point video with interactive streaming of voice, video, and data all at the same time so that everyone in a meeting of any size has the capacity to both view and send animated video as they are talking and sharing applications (which it surely will in the not too distant future), video really doesn't add too much to web conferencing meetings.

But what it lacks in video, Web Meeting Places makes amends for in its ability to automatically format PowerPoint slides into a PlaceWare slide format. Because of this enhanced integration between the PlaceWare format and the PowerPoint format, people can design their presentations in PowerPoint as they normally might and then upload them to their PlaceWare session where they will be translated into the PlaceWare format that provides all of the PlaceWare annotation and collaboration tools.

Been There, Done That

The thing that really makes them different, that really sets them apart, is their longevity and experience in the web conferencing business. Place-Ware was among the first, in the same time frame almost as WebEx, to start to deliver web conferencing to the masses, so they've been at it a long time. And it's their experience that makes them such a good choice for smaller organizations that want or need to use web conferencing to augment their business communications but don't have the time, resources, or money to invest in a lot of self-maintained infrastructure.

For instance, PlaceWare maintains a network of servers that can be accessed by authorized users just about anywhere they can get to a PC and a browser. The network consists of more than 150 servers in data centers located all around the world. The network is redundant with no single point of failure, which means that servers back up other servers and if any part of the system fails in one location, that function will automatically be picked up by another server. It's also load-balanced so that the network knows automatically that if there is too much traffic occurring in one location, some of that work has to be picked up by servers in another part of the network that are not being used so heavily at that time. Having a network with servers all over the world that can look out for one another is not possible for most small organizations with limited resources. PlaceWare takes all the worry out of the technology for them. Most of the other vendors offer this sort of alternative too, of course. But what PlaceWare has going for it due to its long experience working with this technology, is a commitment to maintainability of customers' data in a highly secure environment that most closely mirrors what an organization would have on site if it could. Presenters can upload their content to the PlaceWare service where it resides in a password-protected meeting area until its deleted. While there, it can be accessed from any computer connection.

Another small business aspect of the PlaceWare product that we think they probably developed due to years of experience working with all sorts of clients, is their extensive collection of Customer Guides and Tips. These pages, downloadable from the PlaceWare website, provide in-depth instructions and diagrams about how to use all of the various features of the Web Meeting Place product (see Figure 9.1). These guides, which come in a variety of subjects and are broken down into categories for New Users, Advanced Users, and Administrators, are exactly the sort of help that small businesses need in order to fully leverage their use of web conferencing technology.

Speaking of Help: InterCall's Documentation

In the preface for this book, we discussed our impetus for writing it in the first place. If you remember, it had everything to do with Liz in particular having defined opportunities to use web conferencing, but not knowing how to use it or what it was really; and also not being able to find anything to help fill in those considerable blanks. In other

Figure 9.1.   Web Meeting Place.

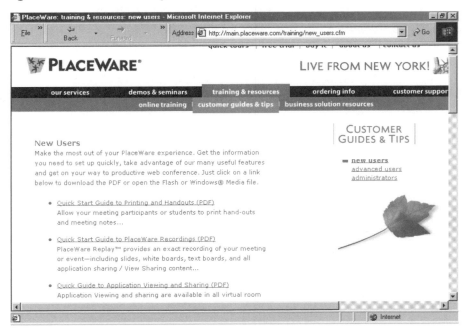

words, the major impetus for this book was the complete lack of helpful documentation about this technology. This dearth of information extended beyond simply not being able to find anything in the bookstores about web conferencing. It went all the way to the lack of helpful, easily discernable information on the websites or in the marketing materials of the various vendors. In other words, as is the case with so many products, the documentation for this stuff is horrible.

Now, people have been complaining for years about their inability to program their VCRs and the documentation for them being of little or no help. But what is sort of a joke or perhaps even a Quixotic Quest for a lot of people where their VCRs are concerned is a matter of serious money where their livelihoods are concerned. This is really what makes the horrific state of documentation so important when it comes to web conferencing. You are going to be asking your organization to put a significant set of resources, including some money, into this technology, and if you can't find good help about using it and using it well, you are going to be up the cyber-creek without the requisite paddle. This is true even if you are a small shop that chooses to partner with a PlaceWare who can help you a great deal with infrastructure.

Enter Present Online from InterCall. This is our example of what downloadable help and guidance should look like from web conferencing vendors who expect organizations, especially small ones, to be able to both fully appreciate and leverage their products.

Present Online and Very Well Accounted For

Present Online is the sister product to InterCall's Meeting Center, both of which are web conferencing solutions that sport all of the features and functionalities that you will certainly come to expect as always available in the web conferencing products that you choose to buy or use. Present Online in particular has bells and whistles such as:

- The ability to surf the web during a web conference
- The ability to record and play back a web conference

- The ability for all participants in a web conference to share applications from their desktop

- The ability to poll participants about the contents of a web conference

- The ability to have multiple presenters who have different authorizations to perform certain functions during a web conference

- The ability to archive documents during a web conference so that they can be accessible after the conference is over

- The ability to whiteboard, or work collaboratively in the web conference's whiteboard space

Intercall also tells a good story in video support via the web, as well as a good strategy for integrated audio conferencing or VOIP. And its Meeting Center product has a lot to offer where document management is concerned. Meeting Center sports great capabilities in being able to share, annotate, store versions of, edit, and share again the sorts of office software documents that people in distributed teams find very helpful.

But their web conferencing solution for small business is not the only reason why InterCall's products are in this book. They are included, and in this chapter in particular, because their way of presenting their product to potential users—especially small business users—is that way that documentation for web conferencing should be.

Intercall makes several documents available on their website. It is called "Present Online Step by Step 5.1." The following is reproduced from that document with permission:

First come their detailed, easy to understand instructions for setting up a meeting:

MAKING A RESERVATION

1. You can make your Present Online reservation online in the reservations section of the website or dial 800-374-2441.

2. Request or select Present Online as an enhanced feature.

3. You will be issued a permanent Owner ID and a Password for your Present Online account.

4. A confirmation e-mail will be sent to you with all of the details for the presentation. (See Figure 9.2.)

Figure 9.2. Presentation Email Confirmation.

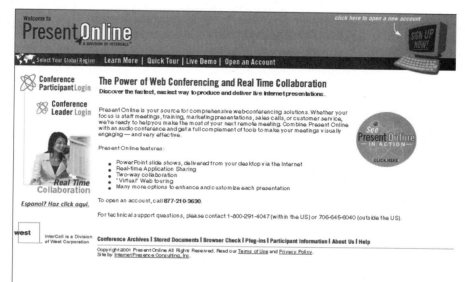

 You may conduct a presentation with up to 49 participants without a reservation.

 We suggest reserving your Present Online calls a minimum of 24 hours in advance to allow enough time to prepare for your presentation.

For Technical Assistance, call 800-291-4047.
Outside of the U.S., call 706-645-6040.

Then comes blow-by-blow instructions for how to get your materials to the meeting site:

LOADING YOUR PRESENTATION

1. Go to www.presentonline.com.

2. Select Conference Leader Login.

3. Enter your Owner ID and Password.

4. From the "Manage your Account" screen, chose Add/Delete Presentation.

5. From the "Add/Delete" "Presentation page . . ." Select Add.

6. Select Browse.

7. Double click on the file you wish to upload. (See Figure 9.3.)

 Make sure "Files of type" is displaying "All Files(*.*)".

8. Title your presentation, then choose a Slide Size from the drop down menu, and click Continue.

Your presentation is now loaded. You're ready to start!

As a leader, you can now dial into Present Online at any time to add, delete, or view a presentation from the "Manage Your Account" screen.

9. You'll be able to see the upload process as it progresses. When you see the words "Your presentation has been added!" in the scroll menu, your presentation has been added to your

Figure 9.3. Uploading a file.

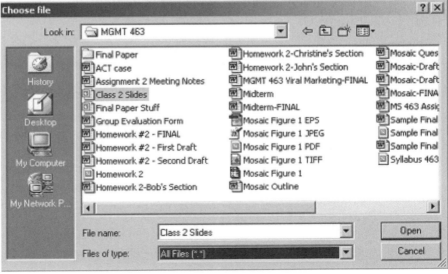

archive. click Continue and then Cancel to return to the "Manage Your Account" screen, OR, click Add to upload another presentation.

Next we find complete instructions for how to get your meeting started:

STARTING YOUR PRESENTATION:

1. Go to www.presentonline.com.
2. Enter as a Conference Leader by entering your Owner ID and Password. (See Figure 9.4.)
3. From the "Manage Your Account" screen, choose Start.
4. Select your presentation.
5. A Welcome window will appear with the unique Presentation Number for your presentation. Give this number to your participants when they are ready to join your presentation.

Figure 9.4.   Establishing a Conference Leader.

If you would like to distribute the Presentation Number prior to your conference, give your participants your InterCall Owner ID with the letter "X" in front of it. (For example, X829279.)

6. Using your telephone, dial into your conference call.

7. Your slides will appear.

For faster slide delivery, run through your slide index before the participants join.

8. Direct your participants to the website at www.presenton-line.com, have them click on the Conference Participant icon. Announce the Presentation Number. For more information, go to the "Joining the Presentation as a Participant" section of this user guide.

Finally, they offer complete descriptions of the features of Present Online, what they are, and how to use them.

CONDUCTING YOUR PRESENTATION

Slide/Panel—Shows the current image being displayed to the audience.

Presentation Number—The number your audience needs to access your presentation.

Slide Index Drop-Down Window—Displays the list of slide titles within the current presentation.

Back and Forward Buttons—To move to the next slide in your presentation, click on Forward. To return to the previous slide, click Back.

Participant Index—The Participant Index shows everyone who is currently your presentation, including names, company names and IP address.

Search Function—Used in conjunction with your Participant Index, the Search function lets you quickly find a participant. Simply type the name of the participant you want to find and click Search.

Make Co-Leader—The Co-Leader functions lets you promote participants so they have the same control over the presentation as you do, regardless of where the participant is located. To make a participant a Co-Leader, go to the Participant Index and highlight the participant you want to promote. Then click the Make Co-Leader button. This person will now see the same screen that you do as the leader. You, as the original leader, can demote a Co-Leader at any time, but they can not demote you.

Dismiss—You can dismiss a participant from your presentation by going to the Participant Index, highlighting the participant, and clicking the Dismiss button. This person should no longer appear in the Participant Index, and will not currently view your presentation.

Preview—Preview lets you privately view upcoming slides. When you click the Preview button, a red border will appear around your slide. You can now click from slide to slide in your index, while your audience still sees the original slide.

Revert—The Revert button is only active when you are in Preview mode. Click on Revert to return to the slide the audience is viewing.

Present—The Present button is only active when you are in Present mode. Click on Present to show the audience the slide you are viewing.

Whiteboard—By clicking on the Whiteboard, everyone can interact (draw, type, diagram, etc.) on an online white board. To return to your presentation, click on the Slides button on the upper left-hand side of your screen.

Chat—Conduct a discussion online. To send a Chat message select the Chat tab and type your message in the Text Box. Determine who should receive your message in the Chat drop down menu and click Send. You can choose from your different modes of Chat:

• Allow Chat—Participants can send public or private messages. Public message can be viewed by the entire audience. Private messages are viewed by the leader(s) only.

- Private Chat—Participants are only allowed to send messages to the leader(s).

- Only Leaders/Co-Leaders—Allows Leaders and Co-Leaders to communicate via Chat while it is still disabled for all other participants.

- Disable Chat—The Chat function is completely turned off.

Q&A—The Q&A function allows your audience to ask questions during your presentation. Incoming questions will appear in the Inc tab. You can choose to respond to questions four different ways.

- Answer—To respond, highlight the incoming question and click on Answer. Your answers will be store under the Answer tab.

- Flag—This function allows you to store questions for lter follow-up. Click on the question and click the Flag button. The question will be automatically moved under the Flag tab.

- Delete—To delete, highlight the question and click the Delete button. The question will be completely removed from Q&A.

- Publish—Publish allows you to share incoming questions with your entire audience. To publish, highlight the question and click the Publish button. All published questions will be stored under the Publish tab.

Polling—Poll allows you to send your audience pre-planned or on-the-fly polling questions. Both types of polling give you automatic results that may be published to your entire audience. To initiate a poll, begin by clicking on the Poll tab.

- PrePlanned Polling—Select preplanned polling questions from the Planned Questions Drop-Down window. Highlight the poll you want to send and click the Poll Button. Your audience will automatically see the polling question and response options. For more information about PrePlanned Polling, go to "Planning Your Polling Questions" in this user guide.

- Polling on-the-Fly—Type your polling question in the Text Box. Select the response options from the Response Type drop-down window and click Poll button. Your audience will automatically see the polling question and response options.

In addition to all of this, this Present Online Step by Step User Guide breaks down all of the functionality of the product in a similar manner. So if you had the Guide while you were first sitting down with the software, it would be hard for you to go wrong. This is great documentation.

Our conclusion is this. We may never be able to get providers of web conferencing (or VCRs for that matter) to produce and make easily attainable good documentation for the products that we buy. But if you're the one in your small company who's going to lead the charge to use web conferencing and you don't have a lot of resources to help you spread the gospel, then you should create a blow-by-blow documentation set for the solution you've chosen. You can then put it on your organizational intranet or on CDs that you can easily ship to whoever needs one. With it, they can fully appreciate what it is you are bringing to them and how it works.

There just no substitute for good documentation, especially in smaller shops.

Linktivity for the Ages

Linktivity is the pair of web conferencing solutions brought to market by SpartaCom Technologies. The products, sort of a mini product suite meant to compliment each other, are Web Demo, their meeting/collaboration product and Web Interactive, their online support product. We'll take a look at Web Demo here.

The first thing that makes Web Demo a good choice for small business is that it is a fully self-hosted only solution; that is to say that you support the software on your own network and not on a network run and supported by the web conferencing vendor. What that also means is that its pricing is simple and a la carte (see the appendix C on pricing). And it's easy to use once you buy it because all of the plug-ins and programs (called applets) you need to run Web Demo are part of the package. It supports email notifications of upcoming meetings and also full Outlook integration so that meetings can be scheduled on all attendees' calendars automatically.

This integration with Outlook is not unusual for such web conferencing products, but what makes Web Demo a good small business choice, beyond the pricing and the all-in-one way it's put together, is that it is a Windows-specific product. It's fully integrated with Internet Explorer 5.0 and up and most notably, its strength is in sharing Word, PowerPoint, and Excel products. The fact is, most small businesses use Microsoft Office Software to run their operations. The fact that Web Demo specializes in using these tools too can be a big plus in terms of familiarity, training, and expense. This doesn't mean that other types of files can't be shared during Web Demo sessions, they can. But if a product does best with that which you use most, there's something to be said for that.

From a maintenance and administration standpoint (technically speaking), Web Demo uses a scheme called ConnectionPoint which actively oversees all online sessions providing secure connectivity that won't interfere with network firewalls. Network administrators can spend less time being concerned with firewall issues. Again, this sort of built-in bullet-proof vest is very important to small shops with limited resources.

Another feature that speaks volumes to small business is the ability, modularly, to add video conferencing capabilities with coordinated Voice Chat audio using Voice Over IP. But what's nice about the arrangement with Linktivity is that you only have to buy and pay for this function if and when you need it.

More Help Along the Way

So Linktivity's product solution is well suited for small business, but it also has a help for small business factor well worth mentioning. They call it Linktivity Systems Integration Services (SIS).

SIS is a team approach to help customers define, plan, execute, and support a successful conferencing and collaboration strategy in your organization. They make sure things fit in existing technology architectures, they make sure that it fits in with existing process (this is likely where the OfficeSuite integration comes in very handy), and they make sure it fits in your budget. It's a smart vendor who doesn't always let money get in the way. Last, SIS remains available to you to make sure that as your business requirements change, your technology stays in step.

The reason that Linktivity can tell this very good story for small business is because it does take a modular approach to the way it delivers its products. That means that its customers can mix and match things as they need them, and if well coordinated, this can be a very effective and cost-efficient way to deliver technology indeed.

Behind Every Great Technology Is . . . More Technology

This chapter is not for the technically faint of heart, but you don't need to know anything that is contained in this chapter to be a user of web conferencing technology. This chapter is really for those who want an understanding of the Wizard behind the curtain. We wanted to include it to give you a good grounding in what the various technologies involved with web conferencing consist of in case you are one of the people who need to understand the details. The rest of our audience may find it helpful to understand terms you've perhaps heard for a long time, but really didn't grasp the meaning or usefulness of. Hopefully contents of this chapter will assist with the implementation of web conferencing at your business or in your home. Please note though that there is chapter 12 coming up about home use that also contains information focused on that use of the technology.

Sometimes the Old Standards Are the Best

In the world of high tech, it is rarely the case that a particular technology stands on its own. So before we get into the nitty-gritty details of the technologies involved with web conferencing, let's take a brief step back and see just what impact technology standards have. This plays an important part in understanding that things are sometimes done the way they are just because established standards dictate that it be so. A good way to illustrate the importance of standards is to repeat what has become a sort of Internet urban legend. It may or may not be true, but it sure is interesting and does speak directly to how standards play a roll in the development and use of my technology.

Where Standards Come From

The U.S. standard railroad gauge (width between the two rails) is 4 feet, 8.5 inches. That's an exceedingly odd number, so the question often is raised, why was that gauge used? The answer is, that's how they built them in England, and the U.S. railroads were built by English expatriates. Why did the English build them like that? Because the first rail lines were built by the same people who built the pre-railroad tramways and that's the gauge they used. Why did "they" use that gauge then? Because the people who built the tramways used the same jigs and tools that they used for building wagons which used that wheel spacing.

Okay, then. Why did the wagons have that particular odd wheel spacing? Well, if they tried to use any other spacing, the wagon wheels would break on some of the old, long-distance roads in England, because that was the spacing of the wheel ruts. So who built those old rutted roads? The first long-distance roads in Europe (and England) were built by Imperial Rome for its legions. The roads have been used ever since. And the ruts in the roads? Roman war chariots first formed the initial ruts, which everyone else had to match for fear of destroying their wagon wheels. Since the chariots were made for (or by) Imperial Rome, they were all alike in the matter of wheel spacing.

So, the United States standard railroad gauge of 4 feet, 8.5 inches derives from the original specification for an Imperial Roman war chariot. Specifications and bureaucracies live forever. So the next time you are handed a specification and wonder what horse's ass came up with it, you may be exactly right, because the Imperial Roman war chariots were made just wide enough to accommodate the back ends of two war horses.

So that brings us to our discussion of the standards that affect the technology we know as web conferencing. Because so many different kinds of technology must come together to support web conferencing functions—like networkings capabilities, video transmission, audio support, data sharing, and remote access capabilities—if the products did not adhere to standards of design and operation, they would not be able to work together and that would make everything else moot.

Acronyms You Need to Know

Any techie worth their weight in code (which actually is more valuable than gold), knows that it is an unwritten law that all engineers must speak fluently the language we call *acronyms*, which is to say that we speak in words comprised of usually no more than three, sometimes four, letters. To do otherwise would allow most normal people to understand what we're talking about. Since you (hopefully) purchased this book, I will break my code of acronyms and explain what all of this mumbo-jumbo means. At the very least you will have lots of acronyms to throw around at your next cocktail party, but hopefully you will also have a good understanding of how the technologies fit into place and you'll be able to apply this new knowledge to your current environment.

Protocols

We'll start from the bottom of the acronym lexicon food chain and work our way up. The bottom of the food chain are the bits and bytes that go across a wire. These bits and bytes are organized into what are called protocols. A protocol is an agree-upon set of conventions used between communicating functional units. A functional unit can be a piece of hardware or software. There are lots and lots of different types of protocols, each one defined for a specific reason.

Internet Protocol

One of the main protocols used throughout the Web is the Internet Protocol, commonly called IP. It is a Department of Defense (DOD) standard protocol designed for use in packet-switched networks.

Packet-switched networks are based on packets or blocks of data, while a circuit-switched network is based on one continuous transmission occurring on a dedicated circuit. The Internet is a packet-switched network; the telephone system is a circuit-switched network. So if you are using networking and the Internet at your office, you are probably using a packet-switched network. At home, your network connection is more often than not going to be circuit switched if you are using your telephone line to get online. This is becoming less and less true, of course, as the number of home Internet users are accessing it with satellite and broadband cable technology. When dealing with IP, the packets that are sent on the network are called datagrams.

IP is responsible for moving packets of data from node to node throughout a network. A node on a network is any device on the network. It could be a server, a PC, a printer, and so on. IP forwards each packet based on a four-byte destination address known as your IP address. IP addresses are maintained by the Internet authorities so that duplicate addresses are not assigned. Organizations then use ranges assigned to them and segment their organizations into departments called subnets.

Communication-Specific Protocols

There are a number of protocols specific to communications over IP-based networks. These standards are designed for point-to-point video conferencing. These protocols allow for file transfer, whiteboarding, and application sharing to take place between two or more communicating parties.

The H.323 standard protocol provides a foundation for audio, video, and data communications across IP-based networks. This of course is how web conferencing is done across the Internet. It is a version of the H.320 Multimedia-over-ISDN standard optimized for packet-based networks such as TCP/IP.

T.120 is another group of protocols for providing the transmission of information in multi-point multimedia communications. It defines the transfer of information in a variety of multimedia applications that can include:

- Data only
- Audio and data
- Audio and video
- Audio, video, and data

TCP/IP

The Internet is based on the packet-switching protocols TCP/IP. Since we already know what IP is (see you are already becoming an acronym expert), TCP (Transmission Control Protocol) is responsible for verifying the correct delivery of data from client to server. It is possible for data to be lost in the intermediate network, so TCP adds support to detect errors or lost data and to trigger retransmission until the data is correctly and completely received.

Networks

Let's take a closer look at the various network types.

PSTN—Public Switched Telephone Network

PSTN is also known as the plain old telephone system (POTS). See I told you, engineers just can't speak like normal people. The PSTN started as human-operated analog circuit-switching systems, the good ol' switchboard with all the wires hanging from it. This ultimately gave way to electronic switches, meaning that the lines could connect automatically and no person needed to move wires around a switchboard. Now PSTN is almost completely digital except for the final connection to the subscriber, which may still be an analog connection.

ISDN

ISDN is the abbreviation for integrated services digital network. An integrated digital network is one in which the same time-division switches and digital transmission paths are used to establish connections for different services. Unlike some other digital communications technologies, like PSTN, ISDN handles all types of information—voice, data, email, fax, sound, and still and moving images. They are all digitized and then transmitted at high speeds in the same flow of data using a single wire, or optical fiber. Optical fiber in particular is capable of carrying different transmissions, up to thousands at a time, synchronously. ISDN works on a group of standard transmission types called channels. B-channels or "Bearer" channels are used for voice or up to 64 Kbps of data, and a D-channel or Data channel is used for call-control signaling or up to 16Kbps of packet data.

PSDN Versus CSDN

PSDN and CSDN are two of the most common types of communication networks. This means that data on the network, in whatever form it takes, will be transmitted either in packets or digitally, depending on the technology adopted by the organization. Packet-switched networks divide messages into packets and each packet is sent individually. There are various algorithms that are used to assemble the packets on the receiving end so that the entire message can be reconstructed correctly. Usually PSDN is fine for communications that don't require real-time transmission such as email. PSDN is commonly referred to as "connection-less" because the route that different packets might take to get to a destination can be different, but eventually they will all make it there.

CSDN, on the other hand, is a type of network that has a dedicated circuit, or channel. The circuit is established for the duration of the transmission. Typically CSDN is used for those types of communication that require real-time transmission. We would not want to have a phone conversation based on packets arriving out of order, so the success of the transmission depends on the characteristics of the network. To that end, a CSDN is sometimes called a "connection-oriented" network.

LAN—Local Area Networks

A LAN or Local Area Network is a communications network that is confined in a limited geographical area, like your home or office building. A LAN is made up of nodes that are connected using familiar terms you might have heard before like Ethernet, Wireless, or Apple's Apple Talk. They are typically used for internal access at a company site. Content that is on the LAN is not usually accessible to others outside your company, even though LANs are usually connected to the Internet because they often are protected by a firewall. If you want to connect more than one LAN to each other, this is done by using dedicated lines, telephone lines, or wireless networks. A group of connected LANs is called a WAN (Wide Area Network), but works on the same principles as a LAN.

Digital Networks

Now that we have a good understanding of the various types of networks, the question becomes how does the network play a role in web conferencing technology? Actually, it plays a rather large role because the success of web conferencing depends on the stability, speed, and reliability of the running network. A digital network offers increased capacity over an analog network so both voice and data can be transmitted; therefore, more information can be sent through the pipe at once. Digital networks also reduce noise on the wire so the stability of the network increases because data aren't being lost or dropped. ISDN and/or CSDN are most commonly used for web conferencing.

Voice Over IP

Voice Over IP, or just VoIP, is technology that allows for telephone calls or faxes to be sent over an IP-based network. The technical challenge of VoIP is to provide a quality of service (QoS) that is equal to that of a PSTN, or a standard telephone network. However, the data you are transmitting is moving over the Internet in packets. Using VoIP can have a substantial cost/benefit to your organization. Deciding whether or not to use VoIP is just a matter of making sure that the technology is ready for your needs. Equipment manufacturers are busily making devices that can support VoIP so that they can get a piece of the substantial pie associated with new VoIP services.

Some of these services might include your local ISP trying to go head-to-head with the well-established PSTN for customers. Think of the savings in long-distance calls that will be had if you could pay a monthly fee to your IP service and can call virtually anywhere in the world for no additional charge. The main protocol used for VoIP is the H.323 protocol that we mentioned earlier.

In Figure 10.1 we see how the office telephones of two remote offices with existing PBX systems can be connected to each other using VoIP. Telephone calls between the two offices are normally made using the public service telephone network, so calls between the offices are at long-distance or international telephone rates. By using VoIP, it's possible to connect the offices without having to go through the PSTN. This could represent substantial savings for the company.

Figure 10.2 shows a generic vendor gateway that provides the hardware and software services required for VoIP. A gateway is just the entry point for accessing these hardware and software services. Obvi-

Figure 10.1. Example office connectivity using VoIP.

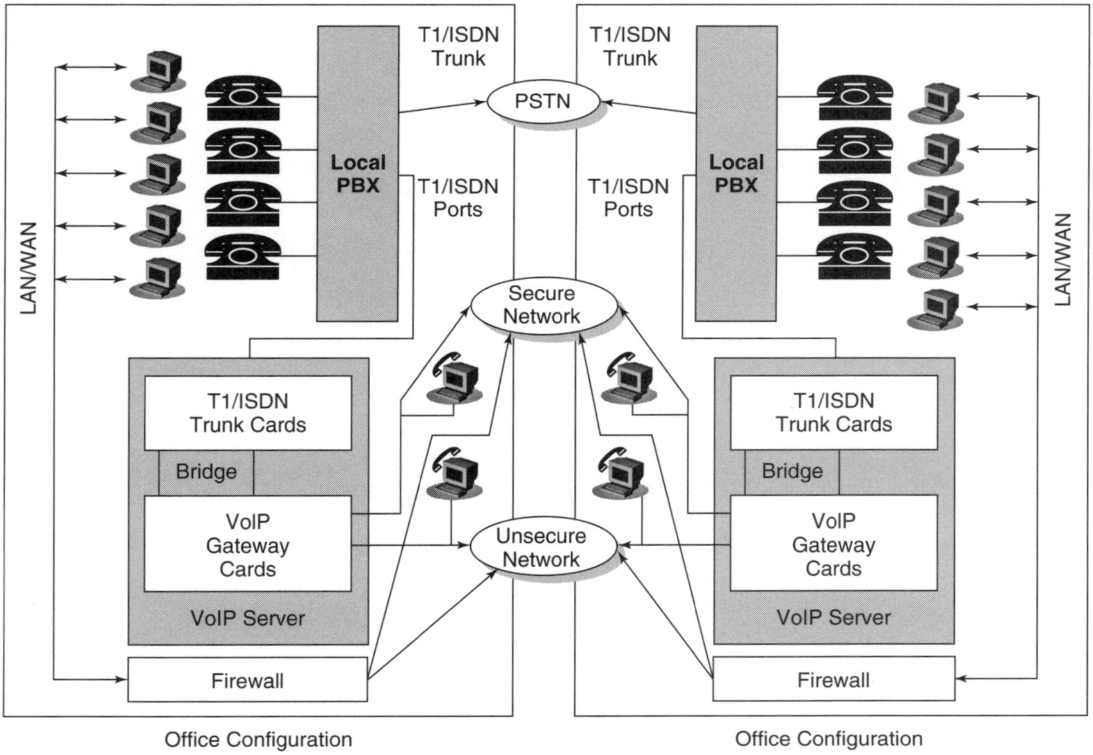

Figure 10.2. Generic vendor gateway for VoIP.

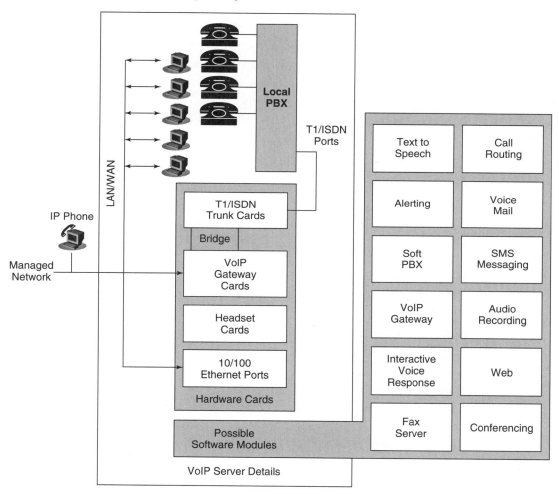

ously there are many options available from vendors and it is your responsibility to understand your requirements.

Security

Dealing with security is on the front burner of many organizations when talking about doing anything external to the organization on the Web. One of the biggest concerns and most frequent question of those getting started with web conferencing is, "How safe is it?" The topics of network security, encryption of data, and user authentication can't be covered here. But what we will look at are some of the common concerns and answer some of the common questions.

Security in most every web conferencing product you'll evaluate is/can be handled at multiple levels. Security can be at the session level where there might be passwords or meeting numbers, and where the host can know in advance who and how many are supposed to be in the meeting. Or it can occur at the transport level, which is where data are communicated. It's here that encoding and encryption take place.

We recommend, make that strongly recommend, that you have an in-depth discussion with your web conferencing vendor of choice to get the latest and greatest details on the specifics of how they are addressing security. If you are evaluating web conferencing for your company, you should probably have an IT person participating in the discussion so that he or she can ask questions that relate to your environment. The last thing we want to happen is that a web conference takes place between participants, and sensitive information that was used appears on the front page of your competitor's site. Don't think it doesn't happen. It does.

We'll assume that, at the very least, your security requirements have two main areas of focus. First, that you want to maintain the integrity of the information used during a web conference. Second, that you want to prevent breaches of confidentiality or integrity. Let's look at each one in turn.

Information Integrity

There are a number of levels that security is dealt with on networks. One is on an encryption level; another is on a functional level. Web collaboration for secure topics should have Secure Sockets Layer (SSL) encryption that provides a high level of data security. SSL encrypts data (using 128-bit encryption algorithms), preventing someone from intercepting and reading the data. Due to a protocol handshake that is performed, SSL can assure a client that they are dealing with the server they intended to connect to as well as preventing any unauthorized clients from connecting to the server.

To put it in terms that most people can understand, when you go to a website to buy something and you input your credit card information, that information will be encrypted using Secure Sockets, which are no more than a type of encryption. The "layer" part refers to where in the transaction this encryption takes place. It's really only of interest to the engineers building the site, but we thought you'd be interested at least in knowing what it's called.

For higher levels of security, the web server must remain behind the company's firewall. This needs to be arranged with the service providers or managed through an in-house IT staff. Functionally, most if not all of the web conferencing vendors require a user name/password login to participate in a web conference. This allows for user authentication and identification as well as for defining roles that each user is assigned within a particular web conference. Obviously this is only as good as the ability of people to not share their user names and/or passwords. Don't overestimate this ability. Most of your participants will leave their user names and passwords on sticky notes attached to the monitor.

Breach of Confidentiality

Usually web conferencing components have very limited access to the resources of the server where they are running. This limitation prevents an intruder from gaining access to other parts of the network. One of the good things about web conferencing technology is that it can work over the same TCP/IP connection as your standard web server.

Most corporations these days have specific configurations set up for their web servers to minimize the risk of breaches. It is a common practice to allow traffic in and out of the web server only on port 80, the standard port for HTTP traffic. Most firewalls are configured to only deal with traffic on this port; all other requests to other ports are denied. This means that the only type of traffic that can get to your web server is HTTP traffic. What this is designed to do is to allow only a single point of access to your organization's internal systems by the outside world, hopefully making it easier to spot hackers trying to access your systems and harder for them to find other ports of entry into those systems.

You should be aware though, again, if you're the person charged with implementing web conferencing in your organization, that sometimes there is a specific port other than 80 that is used for the web conferencing application. If this is the case, it is important to ask the vendor exactly what is going to be accessible to the outside world and how it might be accessed. Only then can you set up firewalls and other security mechanisms to protect your internal systems.

Regardless of which port is being used to access your systems, in the world of web conferencing, usually the web conferencing application has limited access to very specific databases or other pieces of your information that it requires for temporary storage (if needed at all) and nothing else. This translates to a very low risk factor related to web conferencing software.

Equipment You Need for Business Web Conferencing

Phone Lines

Most companies already have what they need to get started using web conferencing. At a minimum all you need is two phone lines (one for audio and the other for Internet access) and a computer with a web browser. Most companies probably have a high-speed connection such as a T1 line or ISDN line anyway, so that reduces the number of additional phone lines required for web conferencing to just one.

Web Cam

If you are the presenter or host of a web conference, you probably also want a web cam (or desktop camera). A web cam (aka PC camera) can be picked up just about any place that sells anything computer-like for between $20 and $100. There is also the plethora of excellent video web cams that can be used to bring live pictures to your web conferencing participants. Many of these cameras can deliver broadcast quality at 30 frames per second and high resolution. Many also have built-in support for protocols like H.320 and H.323, depending whether you are on an IP or ISDN network.

While it's possible for most web conferencing meetings to take place with this minimal equipment, it's also possible that you'll be interested in using more than just the standard telephone and web browser. Let's take a further look at some higher quality equipment so that you can evaluate what's important to your environment and your meeting needs. We'll start at the desktop and work our way to the more snazzy tools.

Desktops

Most vendors support a variety of desktop platforms including Windows, Mac, and Unix. If this is a real concern for you, you probably want to double check the vendors you are evaluating to make sure that your platform is fully supported. If you are planning on being the host, or moderator, of a web conference, you probably want a machine that has a little more horsepower than that of a conference participant. A sufficient desktop for a moderator usually translates into the following requirements:

- A processor that is at a minimum of 233 MHz with at least 64 MB of RAM.
- 5–7 MB of free disk space for the web conferencing application and then whatever is appropriate for your event materials.
- A display monitor that allows for high color definition (16-bit) with the capability to display high resolution, such as 1024×768.
- A standard sound card.
- A headset or microphone, and speakers. You can upgrade to USB digital microphones and headsets that come in stereo so that you can have exceptional sound quality.
- Access to the intranet or Internet.

A participant's machine doesn't have to be quite up to the capabilities of the moderator's. Recommended features include the following:

- A 166 MHz processor with 32 MB of memory
- A standard sound card
- A headset or microphone, and speakers
- 5 MB of disk space for the web conferencing application
- A monitor with a high color (16-bit) display with at least 800 × 600 resolution

Again, these are the typical requirements for a participant's machine. It is best to evaluate the vendor you are interested in dealing with so that you can compare their minimum requirements to the typical setup of your workstations.

Optional Equipment

As with any equipment evaluation, it is always fun to look at what cool toys are available. While most all of the web conferencing vendors will run with the bare bones machines on a 56K modem line, the more you are willing to invest, the more interesting and exciting your presentations (and speed) will be.

Portable Web Conferencing

Now, if you are really itching to have a cool toy for web conferencing here it is. Sony has a mobile video conferencing product called VC VAIO model (PCS-C1XD and PCS-C1VE), which arguably is the world's smallest completely portable H.320 and H.323 compliant video conferencing system. It has a completely integrated PC/VC (personal computer/video camera) solution with camera, monitor, codec, ISDN card, and microphone, all of which are built into a laptop the size of a personal organizer. Simply plug it into an ISDN line and you can immediately communicate with your team, wherever you are. Using this device you can easily incorporate your web conferencing needs and be accessible regardless of where you are. Having one of these in tow is sure to impress if you are on the road a lot.

Wrapping It Up

As you can see, there is quite a lot under the technology covers when it comes to web conferencing. While it is definitely not necessary to understand how everything works to be a user of these products, it you are going to be responsible for evaluating or installing web conferencing, it doesn't hurt to be familiar with the technology. To review, important issues include different types of networks, Voice Over IP, equipment options, and security. At the very least, you should now fully be aware that there are a host of acronyms that you want to be familiar with in order to put all of the pieces in place.

Chapter 11

Computers Don't Use Technology, People Do

People with an intuitive sense about technology and a high degree of comfort with it can be awfully condescending. They'll tell you the ugly truth is that companies have sophisticated technology, but unsophisticated users. Users who just don't get how fantabulous this stuff is. In fact, if you read up on the state of web conferencing on any of the analyst sites or vendor websites or in the archives of the top business magazines, you'll be told time and again that the technology exists for full-bodied collaboration, innovation, expediency, and productivity at minimal cost. The reason it hasn't taken off like a rocket is not the technology's fault, they insist; it's that people lack the skills and willingness to make it work.

Well fear not, non-technologists of the world. Don't feel bad anymore either about your supposed shortcomings, because what the techies are saying about you is only half true. You probably are much better at a skill that they don't give nearly enough credit to: human interaction.

Think of it in terms of the *Wizard of Oz*. The techies are the Tin Men with all the brains; the users are the Scarecrows with a lot of heart. Put them together and hopefully you don't get Dorothy, or worse, Toto. You get optimized performance from regular people at all levels of the organization who are empowered to really use these collaborative tools. And they might even like it.

The Collective Consciousness

So far in this book, we've read about the why, what, and how of web conferencing. Now turn your attention to the "who." Consider the characteristics that humans do bring, can bring, and will need to bring to the party to augment the machine rather than rage against it. What that discussion is really all about is collaboration, and what collaboration is really all about is communication taken to the next level. That is communication with an eye toward getting stuff done. We call it collective communication strategy.

Think of it like this: Audio conferencing was all about verbal expression—speaking and listening to get an idea from one place to another. Once the idea was understood, steps could be taken to do something about it, but the communication method was one dimensional. Video conferencing added the visual dimension to speaking and listening; it put a face or a recognizable object to the topic of conversation. It facilitated familiarity and accessibility, but it didn't do anything to facilitate action. Video just sort of sits there and blinks at you. It's still one-way communication.

Collaborative web conferencing technology has the audio and visual components, but it has something more. It has the tools, built in, that allow you to act on what you are hearing and seeing at the very moment that you are hearing and seeing it. It is not a linear approach to projects or problem solving; it's a collective approach. Not one thing at a time, but rather everything at once.

This approach offers more, but it demands more as well. To achieve more, people need to understand these new requirements so that they can meet them. Most of all, they need to see first that collaborative technology disseminating collective communication is not something being piled on the two hundred mail messages and forty voicemails (both of these also linear, by the way) they get every day. But rather that sooner or later, and according to the self-proclaimed experts (including us, now that we mention it), it's going to replace those one-way communications and things are going to be better because of it. Better in terms of productivity, profitability, job satisfaction, and, dare we say it, even better in terms of taking back control of personal time.

The Way We Learn

According to the Institute for the Future, companies and their workers generate two types of knowledge: explicit knowledge and tacit knowledge.[1] Explicit knowledge is structured and formal, as in an accounting procedure that's put on paper and distributed to everyone in the accounting department. Tacit knowledge is the inferred result of some action that we observe or that we engage in ourselves. In other words, learning by doing. There may not be an explicit policy for how to handle a disgruntled client, but newcomers to an organization might observe that their more experienced colleagues always defer to the client. This teaches them that they are expected to do whatever is necessary to make the client satisfied.

On top of this, the two most effective ways to disseminate information to human beings are visually and kinetically. Visual information is what we can actually see; kinetic information is what we can observe and act upon. Visual information tends to be explicit, and kinetic information is more often than not tacit.

There are four ways in which tacit or explicit information is passed on: combination, internalization, socialization, and articulation.

- *Combination* means that different types of explicit information are combined to create a new piece of information. For instance, you gather all of the HR policies from the various sectors of a company and then rewrite them in a single format to produce a new enterprise-wide policy.

- *Internalization* describes the process whereby people get explicit information from a common company resource, say the company intranet, and then apply it to their own work situation. For example, the organization might put its nondiscrimination policy on its intranet so that all employees are aware of what the expectations are for their behavior toward their colleagues at work.

- *Socialization* is the exchange of tacit information from one person to another. The way a piano teacher teaches a student to play or the way a master carpenter teaches an apprentice to make a cabinet are examples of socialized learning. They are one-on-one experiences in which the student learns by observation.

- *Articulation* is turning tacit information that typically gets lost after it's been disseminated into explicit information that people can understand better and use. In other words, it's not enough for the CEO to tell everyone what the company is going to do to return to profitability because that information can go in one ear and out the other. What's better is if the CEO articulates the reasons for the actions that are going to be taken so that people feel like they understand the whole picture and how it is going to work over time.

According to the Institute for the Future, these methods are less effective when applied to an increasingly distributed and flexible workplace because almost by definition, they demand that people actually be in the same place at the same time to maximize effective transmission of knowledge.[2] In response to that, we theorize that if people apply principles of collective communications instead of linear communications to the use of web conferencing technologies, they will see enormous benefits—personally and professionally. And it will also be possible for people to use information transfer methods like combination, internalization, socialization, and articulation effectively again even if they are working in remote workplaces because web conferencing technology is focused on those collaborative methods.

The Mind and the Computer as One

This discussion of how people acquire knowledge is important to the main subject of web conferencing because how people "get it" (or don't) lies at the bottom of whether whatever technology you bring in-house will be successful in your environment. And by successful we mean more than just realizing the cost-savings benefits of web conferencing. Success happens when web conferencing is embraced

Try This

Recognize that people will need time with the new tools, but as they are adapting to them, gently, slowly (but firmly) remove their access to the old way of doing things. What they're used to is a crutch for them to lean on, so don't yank it out all at once, but do try to make it harder to fall back on.

in your organization to bring out the best in the technology and in the people running it.

So it's crucial that your implementation of web conferencing take the four ways that people "get it" into consideration. If it doesn't, no one will want to or will be able to use what you just invested in. In addition, if you don't understand the fundamentals of people's grasping of new information, you will never successfully expand web conferencing to more and more aspects of your business in order to receive the same ROI that you are probably expecting relative, for example, to your travel expenditures.

Further, without understanding the processes by which people learn things and also pass them along, you can't hope to help them transition from one way of doing things to another. This is different than expanding the use of the technology. This is about people staying in the same job but doing things completely differently. It's the old-dog-new-trick model, and as you introduce new strategies for improving job performance, you are going to find yourself working with lots of old dogs. So as with a real dog, you'd best know what they respond positively to; otherwise, you can find yourself barked at frequently.

Get the Party Started

The fact is that now, in the early days of web conferencing, it's still used primarily for business-to-business communications in which one-to-many is the typical mode. Interaction based solely on technology still feels weird to a lot of people; active participation is offered hesitantly if at all; and complete commitment to the technology without using fall-back positions like travel, email, or the telephone is nonexistent. For example, web conferencing is used effectively for sales presentations, because in a sales call you're used to having someone show up with charts, slides, or demo equipment and you mostly listen and maybe ask the occasional question. If the sales rep is not actually in the room but rather is showing you his wares on your desktop while you're talking to him on a speakerphone, headset, or VOIP, it's going to feel familiar and you'll be okay with it. And indeed, right now people are.

The same applies to mega-broadcasts to thousands of people at once where Bill Gates or someone like him announces his new strategy for world domination. If you hear this, see this, and read this all at the same time on your desktop, then you won't mind not being in the auditorium with a thousand other people in suits and ties who are wondering how this CEO gets away with the jeans and polo shirts all the time. It seems certain he can afford shoes and socks, and yet, he doesn't always seem to feel compelled to wear them. What's up with that?

Anyway, getting big announcements via the desktop seems akin to getting them on the TV or radio, and so we're pretty comfortable with that too. Similarly we are comfortable with PR events or marketing presentations that take place in remote locations. The reason is that sales calls, mega-announcements, PR junkets, or marketing come-ons don't demand a great deal from us other than that we listen, learn, and hopefully, buy. And certainly the web conferencing technology exists to make these events flawless, seamless, colorful, multimedia driven, entertaining, and even interactive.

The Elements of Humanizing Web Conferencing

Here are the elements of web conferencing you must have for people to use it, leverage it well, and finally (hopefully) shout its praises from the rooftops:

1. **Integrate all systems.** Make sure that whatever technology you bring in-house works seamlessly with the technology you are

keeping in-house—not that it works *well* (we'll get to that), that it works *together*. You saw forms of the word "comfort" more than once in the preceding paragraphs, and with good reason. Making people comfortable first and foremost is going to be the foundation of your success. You're already throwing a whole lot of new stuff at them, so the least you can do is make sure the new technology works with the tools they are already comfortable using. Everything should have the same basic look and feel, down to the functionality of the various keys or buttons. The technologies in this book allow for this level of customization in many cases. Use them.

2. **Provide your people with the right tools for the job.** Don't make them invent fixes or work-arounds for equipment that they need to maximize the technology. Make sure, for example, that they can adjust the volume on PC microphones and compatible speakers if you plan on any VOIP. If not VOIP, make sure that headsets are available for their phone units. Otherwise, you will be paying a masseuse to rub the stiff necks of your employees who hold the phone to their ear with their shoulder to free up their hands to use the keyboard and mouse. This might seem trivial, but it's not.

3. **Teach program management.** You'll recall that almost all of the web conferencing technologies we looked at provide some seamless integration to a schedule and document management program like Outlook. Take the time to teach your employees how this integration works so that the first time an employee sees a meeting that she's been invited to on her calendar, perhaps even with an alarm to remind her of it fifteen minutes before it starts, she won't be surprised. Make sure she also understands that she can filter these items and put them in specific places in her calendar or inbox so that she can organize and control them. Control is a very big thing for people just learning these technologies . . . even the ones who are not, by nature, control freaks. Make sure she understands, too, that she can set up her file structure in her calendar and email to incorporate web conferencing communications the same way she may already organize her email folders.

Our View   *When Liz was a New York City high school English teacher, she started*
each of her three semesters without books to distribute to her stu-
dents. For three weeks of every term, she had no books with which to
teach literature. Now you might not like A Tale of Two Cities, *but we*
can tell you beyond a doubt that the book can't be discussed without
being read first. Without the proper tools, Liz could not do her job.
Notice that she is no longer a high school literature teacher. Why do
you care? Unless you want your valued employees to be your ex-
employees, get them the right tools for the job you expect them to do.

4. **Equipment must be as reliable as possible.** Getting back to actual
    hardware, software, cables, and stuff like that, it's crucial that you
    do everything you can to ensure that your stuff is "up" most (if not
    all) of the time. Nothing will kill enthusiasm or a sense of humor
    about starting to do a lot of work via web conferencing than hav-
    ing the system crash on a regular basis.

5. **Get top-down buy-in.** Even if the boys and girls at the top are
    hedging their bets by having another department or division
    under them serve as the experimental lab for web conferencing,
    their complete support for the effort is mandatory. They might
    not be using it themselves, but they (someone from the executive
    suite) should be visible and accessible regularly where it is being
    used, and they shouldn't hesitate to roll up their sleeves and use it
    when in the area.

6. **Ensure accountability.** Make sure that there is at least one person,
    and preferably more than one, in every location using web confer-
    encing who knows everything there is to know about the system—
    from the architectural infrastructure to signing on. Don't fall into
    the trap, as many organizations do, of letting the fabric of account-
    ability get thinner and less responsive the farther one moves away
    from your HQ location or central hub. Next to downtime, not hav-
    ing a resource person there is the quickest way to ensure that your
    implementation is going to crash.

7. **Don't forget the fun.** A very important element of a successful
    transition from old to new is to build in some fun. Now, while it's
    true that people always (despite your best efforts to stop them)

find ways to use the technology for nonbusiness purposes, such as adding to their collection of pre-1950 hub caps on EBay, there is a certain amount of foolishness that should be built into the system in the first place. The downside of this is that not everyone thinks that the same things are funny. So, our suggestion about having fun is to make sure that you control where the fun comes from and what it is. For instance, if you are going to build a training module on how the document management strategy applies to the yearly open enrollment for employee benefits, then you can include humorous jabs at the state of medical care costs in this world (assuming that you can find anything funny about medical care costs). But you get the idea. Or you can use humor in the way that you represent functionality in the interface by using cartoon characters. Be creative with it, loosen your tie . . . unless you're Bill Gates who never wears one . . . and have fun.

8. **Don't be afraid of trial and error.** Pass along your fearless attitude to the people you are encouraging to use the system. If you've done due diligence, your system should have a lot of redundancy or at minimum, a world-class backup scheme so even if something does break, it can be recovered. Make sure your people know that you want them to experiment and explore, and there's nothing they can do short of torching the place that can't be fixed relatively easily.

9. **Make your transition plan and execution participatory.** No one likes to be told what to do, but they do like to be directed so that they feel they're on the right track. Don't have your IT department come in over some weekend and completely overturn existing systems, move everything, upgrade machines, or change interfaces so that the rest of your crew walks into a brave new world on Monday. Plan your implementation to take place during business hours, and to do so without negatively impacting ongoing work; schedule it ahead of time to occur during set hours for set tasks and then stick to the schedule. And better yet, let all those non-techies who are going to be using the stuff help set it up. It will take you longer to do it this way, but the results will be better at completion because you'll have a fully involved, fully onboard, participatory, plugged-in team—physically and mentally.

The Applications of Humanizing Web Conferencing

Now that you've sold web conferencing to the powers that be, you've bought it, implemented it, and transitioned to it, what do you do with it?

1. **Institute training.** Training program design and delivery will be both the easiest thing you can do with web conferencing and also the hardest. Easiest because, as demonstrated in chapter 8 about content design and delivery strategies, there is a whole mess of stuff out there for you to use. Hardest because there is a whole mess of stuff out there for you to use; figuring out which will be best for what training will be challenging. But training via web conferencing is easy because so many of the technologies are created just with training in mind. On the other hand, training can be difficult to move onto the web because people resist giving up the classroom.

 How do you deal with these elements of easiest versus hardest? We suggest two applications: (1) a training course on the technology you've chosen (probably easy enough to get directly from your vendor), and (2) a training course on exactly how to use it. (This will involve more effort on your part because it has to be customized to your environment.) Once you've taken your personnel through these two basic classes, you can broaden your use of the new tools. This strategy will work because the topics chosen for the first two fully conference-run classes are not about anything personal to any employees and also are not about anything performance related. In other words, you're starting them in the shallow end of the pool with plenty of flotation devices.

Try This

Use subject matter experts as trainers, but make sure they also have the personality and skills to be effective trainers. Sometimes people who know a lot about a subject are unskilled in communicating what they know. It's easier to teach good trainers the material than it is to teach unskilled experts how to train.

2. **Conduct work process reviews.** These can be done continually throughout the year using the features of web conferencing. Managers and their teams can share the details of the projects they are working on regardless of how distributed the team is.

3. **Provide feedback mechanisms.** A particular strategy that can be applied to management via web conferencing is MBR, or Managing by Results.[3] This is a strategy that focuses on objective measures of success. Applying MBR to remote employees using web conferencing gives supervisors a way to monitor, recognize, and provide feedback. By the same token, web conferencing is the perfect tool for distributed teams to plan projects—to decide what tasks need be done, who's going to do them, when they will be due, and so on.

4. **Shorten your decision or approval cycles.** Unequivocally shortening these cycles would be a good thing. Web conferencing, with its inherent ability to get all the information to the people who need it, speeds up decision making, and you should think of applying it to that process every chance you get.

5. **Utilize project management.** There is no end to the functions of web processing you can apply to projects huge or tiny, internally or externally in your organization. So, that should be a no-brainer, but don't forget this. Web conferencing applied to projects in your organization allows everyone on your team to see the big picture. Even if everyone working on your one hundred-person project team happens to be in the same physical location, without the document management, desktop sharing, updating, layering, organizing, and recording capabilities of electronic web conferencing, it would be hard for everyone to see the big picture. Letting people see this view encourages input, creativity, loyalty, personal investment, and trust.

6. **Don't get lazy about sales.** Sales is one of the original, most common applications of web conferencing today. One customer of

WebEx's Fugent Communications, which is a communications services provider for the financial market, chose web conferencing as the way to decrease their cost of channel sales. As a result, they cut on-site visit costs by 84 percent while increasing the length of the average telesales call by a factor of ten. How did they do this? They applied all of the functionality, bells and whistles, participatory, and flash and substance capabilities of web conferencing to their sales pitch. They made it *interesting* so people hang with them longer; this allows for relationship building, which generates sales.

Think beyond all your boxes—not *outside* the box, *beyond* the box. We titled this chapter "Computers Don't Use Technology, People Do" in honor of this very bullet. Web conferencing is the closest technology has come and probably will come for quite some time to being able to mimic and provide for all of the intangibles that humans, just by virtue of being human, bring to the collaborative party. Someday we may be able to say "beam me up, Scotty" and someone (it will be remarkable if he is named Scott, huh?) will do it. And someday there will be enhancements to web conferencing capabilities that the engineers are just starting to dream up and put on their incredibly cluttered whiteboards (see Chapter 13 for more about this). But for now, web conferencing can already do more than people know it can. Help them find out by applying it to every business process you have. It won't get saluted every time you run it up the flagpole, but we'd bet it gets that salute more than 75 percent of the time. That's a better winning percentage than the New York Yankees, and that's hard to do without $100 million.

The Skills for Humanizing Web Conferencing

At the top of this chapter, we alluded to the snooty attitude that some technical people have about the capabilities of technology and their ability to understand it all and leverage it well. Show offs. But we also mentioned that non-technologists have basic talents in human interaction that should be nurtured to help engender the most successful use of web conferencing technology.

1. **Personification.** Do you remember this term from high school English literature? Personification is giving human qualities to inanimate objects. Web conferencing is a technical tool designed to improve productivity. But unlike just about every other technical tool, this one is totally about collaboration and working together exactly the way people do when they are face-to-face. This is the first technology that we can attribute human characteristics to because it is simply an extension of human collaboration instincts. Remember, we are social animals. In order to personify effectively, each individual has to think carefully about how it is that he really collaborates most successfully.

   Web conferencing technologies are differentiated from all other technologies by their inherent capacity to take and distribute whatever it is you have to give. Learning how to give is the first skill to master.

2. **Equal Footing.** Web conferencing will not do away with organizational hierarchies. It's not intended to. It's intended to give everyone on a team or everyone involved in any cooperative endeavor equal access to information and to each other within the context of that project, class, or relationship. That's part of the beauty of this technology; it takes people from all over and from all levels and puts them in a place where they can work in true collaboration, but still on their own time, at their own speed, and in their own way. So don't be only a boss; be a facilitator.

3. **Interaction Skills.** These are more than just communication skills, more than just mastery of the art of listening or of conversation. Interaction skills allow a person to exude warmth and involvement remotely.

4. **Place. Learn to understand where you are in relation to the work and encourage others to do the same.** Everyone on your project team or in a class or presentation is going to be at a different place and of a different mind about not only what you are all working on, but also about how they'd like to approach it. Encourage this individuality in both familiarity and working style, and encourage people to continually talk about and share their

Our View   *An excellent example of what we mean by this is illustrated by Liz' first use of web conferencing technology to deliver an e-seminar. She was nervous not only because she was going to be facilitating solely over the Net for the first time and therefore using a subset of her materials designed for that sort of delivery, but also because she was worried about her ability to deliver the course content while involving all of the participants using all the bells and whistles of the software. To make a long story short, the feedback from the group indicated that, while they accepted her mastery of the subject matter and agreed that they'd learned some things, in their overall opinion, she did a poor job of inter-acting with them. This came as quite a shock because in her live ses-sions, Liz typically gets high marks not only for content, but for delivery and putting people at ease and therefore making them feel like valued participants. So, the rest of 2002 was spent on not worrying about the "what" of Liz' web-conferenced seminars; it was spent improving the "how." Specifically, the "how to interact better" when people can see you (Liz uses a PC camera) while basically, they are sitting at a computer with a headset or speaker phone or microphone. To be clearer: How do you make them feel what you are doing as well as see it and listen to it? The answer to the quandary was, of course, inherent in the software, because all of these tools, or most of them, come with user interfaces that have humans completely in mind. So whatever web conferencing technology you choose, be sure that you master it before you go out into the world on it. Understand its capabilities for making you seem more human and accessible and practice using those tools.*

perceptions of what's going on and what they'd like to do about it. Perhaps start every web conferencing session with a status check solely about where people believe themselves to be at with every-thing, and encourage them to use the various capabilities of the software to make their points. This can be enormously effective because it's been found that retention is tied to self-determina-tion and self-policing.[4] People like to be empowered to monitor their own progress, and if there are problems for anyone, then everyone on the team or in the class or program can help.

Try This

In order to improve your interaction skills: (1) use the emotions and encourage the participants to use them; (2) open up the floor for questions at least once every ten to fifteen minutes; (3) for a 1.5- to 2-hour program, develop at least three polling questions in advance and insert them about once every thirty minutes; (4) for classes, develop some "pop quizzes" of four to five questions to be answered in two to three minutes and give participants the results immediately; (5) don't be afraid to add off-the-wall content to your presentations; (6) if others have PC cameras, rotate the video share so that people can see others who want to put themselves up there for a moment; and (7) encourage your participants to send you private chats while the program is going on.

5. **Feedback.** Learn how to give feedback effectively. One of the worst things you can do when trying to institute remote anything in today's workplace is to be hard to find and hard to get feedback from. If you are the point person on a project, or the teaching assistant for a course, or the keeper of the master schedule, or the boss, or even just someone with a piece of information that another person on the team needs, respond to inquiries as quickly as humanly possible. Even if you have to say, "I don't know," or "It will take me a few days to get that together for you," don't make them wait for that answer. Also, if you are in some way the keeper of project status or the developing curriculum, or if you are the person charged with letting everyone know how they are doing as individuals and as a team, then don't be shy about offering feedback proactively. Let people know what's going on and how they're doing even if they don't ask. No matter what you are working on, if you are in some way a point person on something being done in a distributed model, attention to feedback should be job one.

Try This

In order to build trust and help people to bond who are working remotely, try assigning tasks continually throughout the project that involve people in different combinations but that are not too involved and have short turnaround times. This will help instill an attitude of dependability across the group.

To Sum Up: The Results of Humanizing Web Conferencing

What will be the results if you take our advice and pay close attention to the elements, the applications, and the skill sets of web conferencing? You can expect distance to become just another state of mind for the people you work with, and the difference between communicating synchronously or asynchronously across the enterprise to become blurred to oblivion.

And what's good about that? Well, increased productivity, job satisfaction, and profitability due directly to the ability of people to take back a measure of control over their work, their time, and their lives. Human needs enabled with technology. Imagine. And then do it.

Notes

1. Andrea Saveri, "1998 Ten Year Forecast," *Institute for the Future*, p. 167, www.iftf.org.
2. Ibid.
3. Margaret A. Klayton, "Flexiplace: Toward a New Structural Design in Organization" (Fredericksburg, VA: Mary Washington College, 2001), p. 2. www.mwc.edu.
4. Jaclyn Kostner, Ph.D., *Bionic e-Teamwork* (Chicago: Dearborn Trade Publications, 2001).

Do Try This at Home

Chapter
12

The home uses for web conferencing can range from the sublime to the ridiculous. Frankly, we prefer the application of web conferencing to the ridiculous (as we're sure you knew we would). And by this we certainly do mean frivolous or silly or just plain fun. But we also mean creative, energizing, collaborative, sharing . . . and just plain fun.

We bet that many more people are using their PCs for things like doing their banking or most of their shopping than they thought, in their wildest dreams, they would. Everyone we know, regardless of their age, financial status, family status, or profession, who owns a PC or a Mac surfs the Net for information about everything from buying a vacuum to booking a Hawaiian vacation before they ever think of picking up the Yellow Pages or print newspaper.

Within the next five years, many more of these same people will be sending video, audio, and snapshot clips as a regular part of their emails. They'll be creating all of their own greeting cards, making home videos, and getting stuff off their computers at work because they remembered something they were supposed to do before they left the office that they can catch up on at home before they go to sleep.

School projects will be done by young people working together at home instead of simply using the chat programs on their PCs. All of these uses that you think solely as work related are possible now when you apply web conferencing technology to your home PC. This chapter looks at what these uses are and can be, and how it all works.

What We're Using Our PCs for Now

In case you have been losing sleep worrying about whether anyone out there is paying close attention to the way people are using their computers at home, we're happy to be able to put your mind at rest. There is an entire new breed of social anthropologists working for the world's major hardware and software trying to find out what we have done, are doing, and would like to do with the high-tech equipment in our homes. And they aren't limiting their research to those of us who are working at home. They are looking at every family member, even those six-year-olds who have enough technical literacy to scare the feathers off *Sesame Street*'s Big Bird.

According to a recent article in *Newsweek*,[1] these social anthropologists aren't just sending out surveys or calling people in telemarketing style. Instead they are actually going to people's houses, up to ten times in a three- to six-month period, and observing what all the members of the family are doing on the home PC. Then they're going back to their task masters to let them know what's being used, what's liked, what's not, and what people would like to see made available, accessible, and possible on home computers.

Certainly communications capabilities such as chat programs, web logging (personal journals on the Internet that anyone in the world can create and read), and email are the most popular for home users. As folks have become comfortable with these basic applications, their home PC wish lists are becoming more sophisticated. Further, they want these machines to function less like a TV (a device that talks to you while you pretty much sit there) and more like a creative, collaborative, communications tool. Enter web conferencing technology for the home user—a new form of entertainment and expression in the 21st century.

Girls (and Boys) Just Wanna Have Fun

The web conferencing tools covered in this book will work very well for the home PC user. For some applications, however, there could be one serious obstacle: price. Although some vendors have pricing schemes to encourage home use of their products by small numbers of people who might do so irregularly (see appendix C about pricing models), the facts is that this kind of now-and-again use of their products isn't what they have in mind. But there is a product that does have this absolutely in mind, and it's put out by one of the companies who sponsor those social anthropologists you just read about. The company is Microsoft and the product us NetMeeting.

NetMeeting is an excellent choice for web conferencing implementation in the home mostly because, well, it's free. It comes already installed on any machine with a Windows operating system or it can be downloaded for free from the Microsoft site. It's also a good choice because its bandwidth for most of its features is up to eight users.* This is to say that you can chat, work on a whiteboard, share an application, or send files to up to eight people at a time, but you need to be aware that only two of the eight people can have a VOIP connection and/or video interaction. The other six people would have to be on a telephone audio conference and they would not be able to participate using video. Obviously, Microsoft being Microsoft, all of NetMeeting's functionality is completely integrated with the full line of Microsoft products, especially in its latest version 3.01 where it is closely integrated with MSN Messenger, a chat program that most Microsoft users are at least familiar with (if not completely addicted to).

---

*Very technically adept systems people can extend the capabilities of NetMeeting beyond eight concurrent users. This is sometimes done in corporate settings, but it is not the focus of NetMeeting.

Unlike version 2.11 of NetMeeting that was integrated with, but did not demand MSN Messenger, MSN Messenger is now such an integral part of NetMeeting that your use of the web conferencing tool will be negatively impacted if you don't also have Messenger running on your machine. It is not mandatory; it's just highly recommended and it has mostly to do with how you will locate, track, and contact others with whom you want to have NetMeetings. MSN Messenger integration is not the only way to accomplish this; it's just the simplest way. Frankly, depending on the success that Microsoft has in using NetMeeting to leverage its other products (something we're sure they're trying to ascertain from the social anthropologists), they might try to make MSN Messenger integration the only way to contact other NetMeeting users. We don't know this for a fact, we're just guessing.

In this chapter, we're going to examine NetMeeting in some detail. We're going to talk about what it can do, how you can get your hands on it, how to use it, and how you can even use it if you are not a PC user. What if, for instance, you use a Mac at home? What do you do then? We'll tell you.

Accessories like microphones, speakers, sound cards, and PC cameras are optional, but not mandatory, equipment. As with business web conferencing, if you are not using some sort of Voice Over IP scheme at home, you can either have web conferences without any audio interaction or you can just pick up the phone. You don't absolutely have to have a PC camera to successfully use NetMeeting either, because you can receive video whether you have a camera or not. If no one on your NetMeeting has a camera, then there simply will be no video exchange.

NetMeeting

NetMeeting is included in the Windows installation CD that comes with most PCs these days. Or, if the operating system has already been loaded onto a new machine you've just purchased, chances are excellent that NetMeeting is already resident on the machine.

Try This

Please note that there are some significant differences between functionality and operation of NetMeeting v 2.11, which a lot of people have been using for a long time, and NetMeeting v 3.01, which is the de facto standard now. We will specifically point out a major difference in functionality where warranted in our description of the product. If we don't make a distinction between v 2.11 and v 3.01, you can assume we are talking about NetMeeting 3.01, also called "NetMeeting 3."

But what if you're not even using a PC but rather are using a Mac? In this case, you can look into a company called Netopia http://www.netopia.com who has developed a version of Timbuktu Pro to provide NetMeeting-compatible conferencing for the Mac.

If neither of these is true, you can download NetMeeting from www.microsoft.com/windows.NetMeeting. And even if you already have it on your machine in version 2.11 but you want to run NetMeeting 3, you can download the upgrade from the same site. You'll also find downloadable updates, enhancements, and bug fixes on the Microsoft site that you can go and grab any time you like. You'll have to have Internet Explorer (v 4.01 or higher is required for NetMeeting 3) running on your machine. And, for version 3, having MSN Messenger might make life easier, but we'll be getting to that in a little while when we discuss using directories to instigate NetMeeting calls and sessions.

You'll want to remember that Microsoft has never played nice with AOL or Netscape. So if those are your default web browsers and you're looking for NetMeeting-related information on the Internet, you'll have to do a keyword search for Microsoft NetMeeting in AOL or in NetScape. Alternatively, you can do a search on a search engine like Google or Yahoo. If you are running Internet Explorer as your browser, simply typing "NetMeeting" in the browser address box will get you immediately to the NetMeeting page and from there, the links are endless.

Figure 12.1. NetMeeting.

Start It Up

Once you've got NetMeeting up and running, you'll need to configure it. Figure 12.1 shows you how the product first appears to you in a vanilla view.

- **Personal and Directory Information.** The information you have to enter will be your personal and directory information.

This includes things like your name, your email address, directories on your hard drive to which files will be downloaded if you decide to, and so on. This information will allow you to use the software and will also allow others to communicate with you using the software. You enter it by selecting Options from the Tools drop-down menu.

- **Personal Comments.** Comments about yourself are entered in the Comments text box from the Options screen.

- **Directory Service.** This screen is also where you indicate your directory service preferences. NetMeeting assumes that Microsoft Internet Directory is the default directory service that is based on MSN Messenger. Directory services are the things that keep track of user identities on the Internet. There are a lot of them. In order for you to use NetMeeting with another user, you have to be able to find them. In order to find them, NetMeeting will search the directory services that you specify here for the addresses that you tell it to look for. Wait for the subsequent section on directory services for more about how this works.

- **Desktop Information.** You will tell NetMeeting what your modem, DSL, LAN, or other setup is; whether you want to have a shortcut to NetMeeting on your desktop; and whether or not you are using headset/speaker and/or microphone. If you are, you'll have an opportunity to set audio levels before you complete the configuration process.

Once you finish the configuration, the program should start up immediately. If it doesn't, you can start it from the Windows Start program as with any other.

You Make the Call: Directory Servers

Using NetMeeting is pretty easy and it certainly has functionality that closely resembles (ok, copies) the capabilities of other web conferencing software. The hardest thing about it is how to find and connect to the people you want to have meetings with. Once you master this, though, it becomes quite the useful little home buddy.

Technically, there are three ways to initiate a call between you and another user:

1. IP Address.

2. Directory Server located through an ILS (Internet Locator Server) for users of NetMeeting 2.11.

3. Microsoft Internet Directory. If you are running NetMeeting 3, you'll find that Microsoft has replaced its ILS Servers with the Microsoft Internet Directory (MID). The MID can be accessed at www.directory.netmeeting.microsoft.com. It is a website that tracks people who have subscribed to it, when they are online and when they aren't. The MID displays the names/addresses (actually, the IP addresses) of the people in your messenger list as people who are, or are not, currently on line. This is where the MSN Messenger integration becomes important.

Using IP Addresses

An IP address is the logical address of a computer. If an IP address for a computer during a session on the Web was 555.55.44.3, then the 555.55 refers to its network address, the 44 refers to a subnet on that network, and the 3 refers to an individual user on that subnet. IP addresses are assigned by system administrators (on corporate networks for example) or by ISPs (Internet Service Providers) when we dial in from home. Every time you log on to the Net, your IP address is reestablished as being online; so if someone is trying to communicate with you, the directory service will find you and also find that you are online and available for a NetMeeting, a chat, or what have you. Sometimes your IP address will change, but you won't know about it and there's really no rhyme or reason to why, when, or even if it will ever change.

In order to view your IP address while you're online, you can start NetMeeting, choose Help and then choose About Windows NetMeeting and your current IP address will pop up.

So if you want to have a NetMeeting with a friend, or up to seven friends, you could ask them to call you while they're online and tell you their IP address so that you can call them to start a meeting.

Once you have this information, you click Call (refer to Figure 12.1) and then New Call. You will see a "Place a Call" window and you enter the IP address. If it's an address you've called before, you will be able to click on the address in the "To" pull-down menu. The person you are calling will see a pop-up window on her screen indicating that there is a call from you (it will tell her who's calling) and she can choose to accept or ignore the call.

If you both have sound cards and microphones (speakers and/or a headset would help too), then you can also speak to each other during the session. And, if you have video cameras, you can also see one another.

Once you're connected, you can bring up to six more people into the NetMeeting. although in the scheme we've described here, since you're also doing audio and video with the first connection, you will be unable to do either with any of the other parties. Those users would communicate with each other, and the first users would communicate with them, using ancillary telephones or via an online chat that is also part of NetMeeting.

Using Directory Servers

In order to initiate a web conference using directory servers, the first thing you need to do is determine to which directory server you are connected. Again, the directory server, like the Microsoft Internet Directory that we described earlier, tracks the names and IP addresses of people as they access the Internet. If you are running NetMeeting 3 and MSN Messenger, then the Microsoft Internet Directory will be the easiest to use and will also likely appear as the default in the Directory Settings screen, which is also located in Options/General.

Microsoft used to support and list a great number of ILS servers, but with NetMeeting 3, as we said, they prefer that you use the MID. Whether you use ILS or MID, the directories serve the same purpose. You can select a directory when you start NetMeeting, or you can set a preference for your machine to automatically log on to your directory every time you start NetMeeting. By logging on to the ILS server you are indicating that you are online and that you are at a certain IP address. Now people who want to initiate a NetMeeting with you only need know the ILS server you are logged into and your email address.

As an extra level of security, you can log on to an ILS server and decline to be listed in a viewable directory that anyone who goes to that directory can see. But if people you know and trust want to find you and they know the server you're on and your email address, they will be able to search for you specifically to see if you are online and therefore if they can initiate a session with you. This is not too much different from how AOL's Instant Messenger works, but you can't share files, video, and so on with IM.

As we said, the MID is the directory server that Microsoft would like to see you use, and it is the de facto choice in NetMeeting 3. But if you are using NetMeeting 2.11 and you don't want to download the free upgrade because of how buggy or unstable these new releases can be, or you simply want to use other ILS directories, you still have choices.

The Microsoft NetMeeting homepage has links to lists of ILS servers. Or, if you enter ILS or ILS.servers in a Google or Yahoo search, you'll get a lot of them that will look something like this:

www.ilscenter.com

ils.worldonline.nl

ils.vocalscape.com

ils.onlink.net

ils.netmeeting.co.uk

ils.glorb.com

ils.glazier.co.nz

ils.council.net

ils.ctdepot.com

ils.chi.town.com

This is by no means the definitive list of ILS servers in the world. (See Figure 12.2.)

Figure 12.2.   This is what the search page of a typical ILS server looks like. This particular screen comes as the result of using the Intel Directory Server, which loads when you use Create & Share software for your PC Camera. We'll be looking at that product more closely in this chapter.

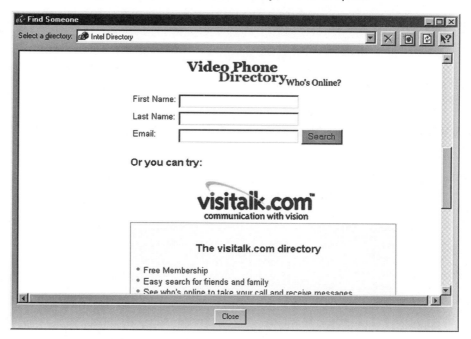

When you select a directory and access it, you will be rewarded with a list of your contacts who are also online and are logged into the directory. If you double click someone, they will get a pop-up box indicating that you want to initiate a NetMeeting and again, they can decline or accept.

Using MSN Messenger

If you are using MSN Messenger, then your contacts and their email addresses are already established in your contacts list. You simply right-click on a name, choose invite, and an instant message alert will appear on both of your screens. Again, the person you are calling can choose to accept or decline the invitation.

Why All These Choices?

Obviously, the simplest of these methods is to use NetMeeting 3 with MSN Messenger and simply enter people's email addresses that you can cut and paste or simply pull from Outlook. But what if you are not running the latest versions of everything or you don't want to subscribe to MSN Messenger? Then the ILS servers and the Microsoft Internet Directory offer you options, as does the call by IP scheme; you just have to know more about your intended collaborators in advance.

What You Can Do with It

Once loaded, configured, and your directory scheme is set up, you have a fully functional web conferencing application. Among these functions are:

- **Advanced calling** gives you the flexibility to send a mail message to a NetMeeting user or to initiate a NetMeeting call directly from your mail address book. This resembles the integration of the office-based web conferencing systems with Outlook.

- **Chat** allows you to have real-time conversations using text with up to eight people. The ability to have a more private conversation with one other party in a NetMeeting is called "Whisper Mode." You can also save the contents of a chat session to a file for future reference. This is similar to the ability to record web conferencing sessions.

- **File transfer** lets you send files during a NetMeeting. You can send a file in the background, send it to everyone at once, or send it to one or more—but not all—participants. Participants have the ability to accept or reject files.

- **Program sharing** enables better control over how shared programs are displayed on your desktop, and it gives the person sharing the program control over who uses it. You have a great deal of leeway over how you view shared files. They can be in a frame, in a minimized window, or in a full screen. There are quite a few options you have for who can share your programs and how they can (or can't) manipulate them. If you are concerned about letting people access your desktop in this way, just keep your finger planted near the "ESC" key. If someone starts messing around beyond your liking, hit it and you will have control of your computer again.

- **Remote desktop sharing** lets users call a remote computer to access its shared desktop and applications. This is a rather nifty feature that lets you access your PC at work using a secure connection and a password to access the other machine and your files. Obviously, the security considerations here are many and varied, but NetMeeting does use data encryption, user authentication, and password protection strategies.

- **Whiteboard** lets you collaborate in real time with others using graphic information, exactly as it does in the business-oriented web conferencing programs with all their horsepower. You can even load saved whiteboard pages in advance of a NetMeeting and then drag and drop them into the whiteboard during it. (See Figure 12.3.)

Just a Word About Security

Security is a new feature in NetMeeting 3. We guess the world was a less threatening place when v 2.11 was around. Despite trepidations you might have about doing the upgrade, or your desire not to give up your use of your ILSs in favor of Microsoft Internet Directory, the security features of NetMeeting 3 might be a compelling enough reason for you to do the upgrade anyway.

Security in NetMeeting appears as:

- **Data encryption** that encodes data exchanged between shared programs, transferred files, chat, and whiteboard. You can specify whether all secure calls are encrypted, and you can have secure conferences where all data are encrypted.*

*Audio and video must be disabled.

Figure 12.3. Figure 12.3 shows the icons for the various capabilities of NetMeeting. Along the bottom of the figure, the commands are (left to right) share program, chat, whiteboard, and transfer files. The buttons on the right (top to bottom) are place a call, end a call, look someone up in your directory(ies).

- **User authentication** verifies the identity of participants by requiring authentication certificates. Such certificates are automatically generated during NetMeeting setup.
- **Password protection** means that you require a password for anyone to join a meeting.

You Oughta Be in Pictures

Some of the most fun things you can do with web conferencing at home occur when you partner the conferencing software with some of the available PC camera software and then get all messy playing around with it.

Now, on the Internet you can find myriad lists of different kinds of cameras, speakers, headsets, and microphone setups to indulge in. And if you research each of them, you will learn about clarity, bandwidth, resolutions, and so on. But for our discussion of what's available to the home user that combines the best of PC camera capabilities with web conferencing, in this case NetMeeting, we chose the Intel PC Camera with the Intel Create & Share software.

Leaving aside the communicative/collaborative aspects for a moment, the camera enables you to:

- Take snapshots and then file/save, print, or email them.

- Record video and audio and then make email or video greeting cards that you can send to people directly or incorporate into a NetMeeting.

- Create and share photo albums online.

- Use a digital camera independent of your PC or a scanner to import images into the program that you can then work with and share as you do images taken with the PC camera itself.

- Create your own homepages on the web.

- Interact with computer programs in a virtual reality scheme that allows you to insert yourself or others into the flow of the program. These are really sort of silly games. There's one where you use your mouse to bounce a ball around a large room. Using your camera, you can insert an image of yourself into the room and bounce the ball off your head. Pointless, but strangely, quite amusing for short periods of time.

Let's take a look at some of what Create & Share can do, starting with integrating it with NetMeeting.

The Create & Share Program

If you have NetMeeting and MSN Messenger both running on your machine along with your Create & Share software, which is the software that controls the Intel PC camera, you can initiate a NetMeeting session from the NetMeeting call screen simply by typing in the email address of the person, or persons, you want to meet with. This assumes that you have entered their name and address in your associated Microsoft Internet Directory or that they are already in your email address book.

If not, you can still initiate a NetMeeting independent of Messenger and of NetMeeting because NetMeeting is part of the Create & Share program as an independent program. It also accesses a directory server maintained by Intel that is called, to no one's great surprise, the Intel Directory Server.

Last, if you don't have NetMeeting or Messenger and you don't want to log on to a directory server, you can still call other computers by accessing them by their IP address from the call screen in NetMeeting that you get to through Create & Share.

So, in short, NetMeeting calls work the same as an adjunct to a program like Create & Share as they do otherwise.

The Gallery Rules

The Gallery is the heart of the Create & Share software, the place where you organize all of the files you are using in your home web conferencing. For example, let's say you just took a great vacation and you have uploaded your pictures from the trip onto your PC. Now you want to share them with friends, so you move them all to a file folder in the Gallery called "our trip" and you can show them to your friends while you're online with them.* You use the Gallery to save, organize, and open projects or files, and your active Gallery will appear as the default home screen on the left side of your home screen when you open up the software. (See Figure 12.4.)

---

*"Media" in this instance referrs to snapshots, video, or audio files.

Figure 12.4. The Gallery appears as a pull-down menu item on the top task bar or also as a searchable field in the upper left-hand corner. The same files can be accessed either way.

You can have any number of galleries; think of them simply as file folders. The Gallery on your home screen is sort of like the filing cabinet in which all of the other galleries are stored. To access files in another gallery, simply click on the one you want from the pull-down menu that appears when you click on the homepage Gallery. Again, this works exactly the same way as selecting files in Windows does.

In addition to being the file cabinet and sorting mechanism for your media files, the Gallery is the place where you can do simple editing of your files and is also where you can ascertain the properties of your files. For example, the properties of a still image file might be its name, location, file size, or resolution, while the properties of a video file would include all of that plus how many frames there are and what their speed is per second, among other things. An audio file's properties could include its name, location,

Figure 12.5. The user interface.

size, and format. All of this information is important if you are going to transfer any of your media files to other mechanisms of manipulation or transference such as one of the online print and manage services like Ofoto (see Appendix B) that are available to you via the Internet.

In Gallery, the simple editing you can do is to adjust the brightness/contrast of an image, crop it, or rotate it (usually for printing purposes).

The homepage of Create & Share presents you with the options as noted in Figure 12.5. We found that regardless which you choose, the user interface is extremely friendly. Once you've set up your Gallery file structure, it is a piece of cake to create, edit, and send images and audio clips via your email or over the Internet.

Of particular creative potential is the ability to create your own homepage on your own website on the Internet. The software, although simplistic, has myriad opportunities to create different pages, links to

Figure 12.6. Create & Share offers templates to build homepages with. The one in Figure 12.6 is designed to be for a homepage of the user's family tree. There are dozens of templates to choose from in the program.

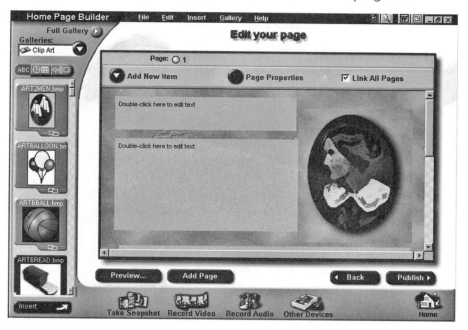

all those pages, and also hyperlinks to other pages on the Internet, whether they be yours or someone else's (see Figure 12.6).

When It's Not All Fun and Games

Hopefully you've gotten idea that you can do a great deal of a collaborative and/or creative nature on your PC at home using tools like NetMeeting and a PC camera with its associated software. In fact, it took Liz three days longer to write this chapter than it should have because she spent so many hours sending email postcards, videos, and audio clips to her friends and family. There's an excellent chance that they'll either get these tools themselves, or that they'll be flying immediately out to Colorado to throw Liz' PC out the window.

But for some reason that we've yet to come to truly understand, it can't be fun and games all the time. Sometimes you have to get serious work done even in the comfort of your own home; the PC with collaborative software has become a means to accomplish that too.

There are lots of examples of this. For instance, in Colorado, the University of Colorado and Colorado State University have put aside the differences that typically manifest on the football field to create a statewide initiative called "Bridges to the Future—American History and Values in Light of September 11th" (www.bridgestothefuture.us). These two schools, along with other Colorado foundations, funds, and the *Denver Post* and *Rocky Mountain News* have created a framework that will manifest itself through live events, cyber events, instructional opportunities, and essay contests, to name but a few of the mechanisms. This framework is entirely designed to let people share their thoughts, feelings, and observations about the United States as an entity and also about its place in the world, post September 11, 2001.

The idea is that by using the vast collaborative capabilities of web conferencing technologies, people will be able to participate in, write about, view images and videos of, and listen to the observations of others in such a way as to forge new understandings and new strategies for dealing with an increasingly volatile and challenging world.

This is the essence of education: the communication and sharing, the processing and consideration of ideas and concepts. It is a perfect use of the capabilities of the Web and web conferencing and speaks directly to the criticism of some that say that our exploding use of technology is actually a depersonalizing, alienating force on the planet. Perhaps in the strictly linear models of email and bulletin boards this is a valid concern, but in the realm of truly collaborative tools and innovative application of them, it is not. Used correctly, the Web and web conferencing can be an enormously positive tool in bringing people together.

Another example of this is how local governments are moving beyond simply putting all of their "stuff" on the Internet, and are now utilizing web casting as a way of bringing government closer to people and encouraging and enabling public participation in government.

An example we read about is in Cupertino, California. This is a city that recognizes that 90 percent of its 50,000 residents are online[2] and that this degree of connectivity represents a huge opportunity to instigate involvement. So now all of Cupertino's municipal meetings, like city council and planning board hearings, are being web cast using technology from e-StudioLive. All residents have to do is surf on over (and they just love surfing in California) to www.cupertino.org and they are participating in their own lives.

School Daze

But certainly the most prolific use of the home PC for collaborative projects that are not strictly for fun is its exploding use as a means to get an advanced degree. Frankly, there is not a single school that is not offering some portion of its courseware, including in some cases the entire curriculum requirements for a given degree like an MBA, over the Internet. And of course, in order to participate, you need basic web conferencing capabilities and equipment (see Chapter 9 for what "basic equipment" means).

When we first developed the outline for this book, we thought we'd be listing institutions of higher education that you could investigate online degree or professional certification programs with. In reality, such a list would comprise a book all of its own. Suffice it to say that there isn't a school you could look at right now, from Harvard to UCLA, that doesn't offer online curriculum, distance learning mechanisms, and degree programs. So if that is your interest, you will have no trouble whatsoever pursuing it.

E-Learning Still in Kindergarten

Despite its popularity, which in fact might just be a misnomer for its rampant availability, you should know that e-learning for formal education still has some bugs to be worked out, especially when applied to undergraduate and secondary schools' usage.

In the State of Colorado for example, there has been a big push for e-learning, especially in those places (and there are quite a few out here) that are so rural that getting teachers for more esoteric subject matter like foreign languages or economics is difficult. Just general teacher shortages make e-learning schemes attractive to districts that are far flung and lack all sorts of resources, but who do have access to PCs, electricity, and phone lines or even satellite or cable connectivity options.

These alternatives strategies are positioned as being teacher led, collaborative, and standardized so as to conform to the state education requirements; and they are, but they are not without difficulties that have nothing to do with their design or content.

According to a piece in the *Denver Post* on April 28, 2002, high attrition rates in e-learning schemes at the secondary school level are due mostly to the fact that people think that online courses are going to be easy, but they are no easier by design than a regular class is. They might actually be harder because although the software is collaborative and the courses are interactive, people are still working in what feels to them like isolation. They don't seem to believe that there are really other people "out there" when they're online and this makes them feel alienated from the effort. As a result, they don't perform as well as they do in "live" classrooms.

This is not to say that there isn't a future in online learning. Like it or not, there definitely is, especially as the next generations of people come of age by growing up with the PC as a tool more collaborative, less linear, and more intrinsic to their daily lives. For the time being, it is interesting to us that the people who will likely get the most benefit out of distance learning and online degree or professional development programs for the three to five years will be older people. What they lack in technical sophistication as compared to their children, they more than make up for in self-discipline and the ability to work singularly.

Notes

1. *Newsweek* (October 21, 2002), p. 67.
2. "WebCasting: Government for the People," *eWeek magazine* (March 11, 2002), p. 3.

Ready or Not, Here It All Comes

Chapter 13

This book has covered lots of ground examining what web conferencing is all about. We've looked at what it can do to immediately impact the way you interact with just about everyone. Now it's time to take a look at the ways in which web conferencing will strive to expand your horizons in all sorts of ways . . . sometimes whether you want it to or not.

One of the fun things about being involved in the high-tech industry and actually having the opportunity to build the technology, is that you—or in this case, we—know what's coming down the pike a year or two ahead of what the rest of the world who is not so directly involved in development sees. I have a confession though. Most of the time even techie geeks don't really know what all the uses are going to be for the technology we're putting out there. That's where all those revisions to software are born.

So in this chapter Liz and I take a look into the crystal ball on the desk (ok, so it's really a paperweight) and tell you what we think is going to be available, the types of technologies that are going to play a role in the things you do relative to web conferencing, as well as a stab at imagining the kinds of applications that are strangers to us now, but will be common in our lives soon

Emerging Communications

Current web conferencing technologies can be categorized into three groups: e-learning, web meetings, and web seminars. These applications for web conferencing include products for web events, VoIP, web seminars, chat and instant messaging, meetings, and learning-focused tools.

One of the trends is that these web-based enterprise communications tools are going to merge into integrated platforms so that many (if not all) of these solutions will be available as a single solution. Will this be the so-called "killer-application"? We'll see. People have been promising to deliver the one-stop-for-everything-killer application since software was born, but it hasn't happened yet. Something is always missing. When web conferencing becomes woven into the fabric of our daily lives to the extent that email is today, then we'll know if the killer application has emerged.

In the meantime, there are compelling technology strategies teetering on the edge of being the ultimate solutions. They're only waiting for some of the other technologies upon which they are dependent to break through so that they can become ordinary in our day-to-day work and home communications lives. Let's take a look at what some of those technologies are, and the types of solutions that are emerging.

The Need of Speed

If there's one thing that you can never have too much of, it's speed. In the world of software and communications technology, speed can manifest itself in a variety of ways. Speed can be part of the hardware you use, part of the software's performance, or a result of the type of Internet connection you have. No matter what it is, and it's usually all three, there is always a need for more speed.

So, in this never-ending quest for faster, faster, faster, one of the technologies we should see giving a boost to the world of web conferencing is compression technology. Compression means the ability to send more data, video, sound, and so on using less bandwidth or physical space on the wire and doing it faster. Improvements to performance relating to compressing data applies to all users of collaborative technologies, both at home and at work.

The compression of data on the network will allow for an exciting explosion of high-end multimedia in web conferencing. We'll have the ability to share video and audio communications in conjunction with conferencing that is so fast that it will seem as though the people you're communicating with are in the room with you. This greater speed of transmission will make for a higher quality user experience because the human interaction will be really real time, and not just the sort of fake real time we're all operating with today.

Applications will go way beyond meetings. We talked in this book about how we believe the next real explosion of fully leveraging web conferencing software is going to be in the e-learning realm. What's coming down the road in terms of video and audio compression technologies is going to play a big part in making distance learning take on the in-the-classroom feel that it needs to really catch on with people. And that's just one example. Here's another.

Imagine being able to deal with a travel agent in a web conference, telling him places you'd like to go and the things you'd like to do. Your travel agent can, on demand, load video of various places that you might enjoy and you can view it while the agent talks about it. Heck, you can be viewing it at the same time your agent has conferenced with his counterpart at her office in that location who really knows the place and you can all be on the same virtual tour at the same time.

Media on the Web—The Rich Get Richer

This type of content, made possible by compression, will make business-to-business applications more interesting as well. As a sales representative, you will be able to contact a potential (or existing) customer via a web conference and take them through a virtual, rich media experience all about a new feature of your product. The efficiency of what you'll be able to accomplish will be enormous.

Rich media capabilities will be built into customer relationship management software. The web conferencing will be another component of how the relationship is managed and supported. And speaking of support, being able to resolve problems with customers while on web conferences, all happening at a blink of an eye, will certainly create a more productive environment for customers and vendors to interact in.

And Here's What's in It for Them

Another example of rich media value made possible by more powerful, faster connectivity capabilities is from the consumer's point of view. Sometimes this is referred to as the customer experience management, or CEM. Say you want to buy a new car, but don't want to deal with the car salesperson. We're not sure if there is anyone who actually wants to deal with a car salesperson . . . not even another car salesperson.

As a potential customer, you want to investigate numerous cars before deciding what you really want to buy. Instead of driving all over yourself, the dealer now has web conferencing set up so that you can first take a look at the rich media presentation of potential product choices with salespeople answering your questions live. So once you locate a vehicle you're interested in, you have the option of customizing it in real time. You can chose the color you want, interior, wheels, and options while the salesperson inputs your selections and produces a video image, in 3D and from several views right there on that web conference—all done at your convenience. It will be much easier to bounce from vendor to vendor through your browser than it will be to go to each of the dealers in person. And when they give you the line about having to discuss something with their manager, you can log off and surf elsewhere, taking all of your vehicle specifications with you.

Using compression technology will also make it possible to do interviews via web conferencing. Human resource organizations will be able to set up web conferences with potential candidates and have any number of people at a company involved with the interview process through a single session. The interviewee will be able to supply voice as well as video to the potential employer, even if they don't have high speed Internet connections and thus enable an interactive interview process.

Can You Hear Me Now?

Voice-enabled applications will also personalize the web conferencing world. We'll be able to pass a web conference along from person to person as part of a workflow. Here's an example.

Let's say that you are involved in Enterprise Resource Planning (or ERP). You should be fully aware by now that every concept in the English language actually has an acronym already assigned to it by someone in the high-tech industry. Sometimes Sue thinks that she only really knows how to speak in three letters at a time. But that's another story. Back to ERP. Typically there is some type of supply chain within a business. For example, a purchasing department might deal with purchasers and their requisitions, vendors, and project managers. Using a voice-enabled ERP system, web conferences will take place with the people involved in the supply chain. When the next group of people need to be involved, they will be notified that there is a web conference waiting for them and the hand off to the conference will be done by voice activation.

In this book, we've talked about Voice Over IP, and that's just the beginning. Soon we'll see PDAs that have mobile phone capabilities as well as video. Using a wireless connection to get access to the Internet, you'll be able to log in to a web conference and transmit video while holding your PDA in front of you. If will likely be possible to have integrated voice recognition where you can voice command a web conference to take place, and have the PDA connect and activate the video for you. Cool!

Mobile Conferencing

This leads us to the land of mobile conferencing. The mobile landscape is on the verge of exploding. For many years, we have been inundated with marketing propaganda about how everything will be in the palm of our hand. Well folks, the time has just about arrived. There are many—some say too many—gadgets available on the market now that can connect, dial, ring, schedule, and do just about everything that you could possibly think of. PDA sales are projected to surpass $20 million by 2008.

Using a PDA like the iPAQ from HP, it is possible to run from the airport to your client's site carrying nothing more than your iPAQ in your pocket . . . and maybe a toothbrush. Let us explain why.

An accessory for any iPAQ is an expansion pack, which is a case that the handheld device fits into; expansion cards (they look like credit cards) for communications and presentations plug into the expansion pack Armed with Bluetooth, which is a wireless connectivity software protocol that the latest and most expensive handheld models come with, your iPAQ can now communicate, wirelessly, with your other technology toys that are Bluetooth enabled. Think of Bluetooth as a radio, one that sends out a frequency to other devices like your cell phone, laptop, PC, or even your printer, and receives signals back from it. Those frequency signals allow those devices to now interact with one another using the iPAQ, running Bluetooth, as the middleman.

For wireless connectivity to the Internet, this means that you can connect to the Net from anywhere on the planet you can find a Bluetooth-enabled gateway. For instance, there are kiosks in airport terminals and in PC cafés now that have Bluetooth-enabled connectivity. You simply load that device (it could be a PC or a phone) into your Bluetooth manager's software on your iPAQ and you've establish a wireless connection to the Internet.*

And there's another way you can establish a wireless, mobile connection to the Internet using just your iPAQ and your cell phone. A company called BVRP introduced a new technology for turning cell phones into modems for surfing the Web wirelessly on a laptop or PDA. This has been possible in theory for a long time,

---

*Please note that we are talking about the physical connection here. You would still need an ISP to dial into or your corporate LAN to access your email or files.

but actually doing it required getting to a number of different providers and implementing various technologies from each to get it all to work together. The BVRP product cuts through all that technical red tape and enables a user with a phone or PDA that has Bluetooth wireless technology to simply press "connect" and surf the Web wirelessly.

Now those of you who have heard of, or are even perhaps using, Wi-Fi which is a new technology that allows people to pick up on (what is called "beaming to") Internet connections that are floating around in space, you might be wondering what the difference is between Bluetooth and Wi-Fi. Right now, and for the immediate future, Bluetooth is better for mobile devices because it uses less power. Wi-Fi is fast and its has great range, but it is also less reliable in its current state.

Life Without a Net

Well that's all well and fine for the mobile market, but how does that play in the web conferencing market? Glad you asked.

So there is a Bluetooth wireless network that allows you to seamlessly connect to the Internet via your cell phone and your iPAQ. You can also access a web conference that is taking place with one of your customers who is deciding whether or not to purchase a large quantity of product from you. This customer would like to see the value proposition of doing business with you in the future. What you need is a way to show them your sales presentation again, with all its cool graphs and charts, right then and there.

Luckily for you, your iPAQ comes with presentation software called iPresenter (www.ipresenter.com). This software enables you to take a PowerPoint presentation off your PC and load it on the iPAQ before you leave the office. Now you can view it on the iPAQ or pull it into a web conference on the fly, just as if you were sitting at your office PC doing the sales pitch. It simply appears as just another file in your file explorer, and if you need it, you click on it so that everyone on the web conference can see it. And all this is happening while you are sitting in an airport waiting for a flight that got delayed.

Not Pure Web Conferencing, But . . .

This next point is not pure web conferencing capability, but as road warriors, we would be horribly remiss if we didn't mention another way that you can use web conferencing and your handheld to avoid lugging that laptop everywhere. We discovered this capability while investigating whether or not web conferencing is available to mobile devices (it is) and we just wanted to share it.

Not only can you use iPresenter to run your presentations on your iPAQ, you can also use your iPAQ instead of your laptop to project your presentations using a VGA monitor projection system to live audiences. This is made possible by using a Compact Flash VGA card like to one we got from Colorgraphics (see Figure 13.1).

All you do, if you've purchased and expansion pack for your iPAQ that will only run one external card at a time (it's possible to get a two-

Figure 13.1. This shows you what the Voyager Flash Card looks like and also lists the product's specifications.

slotter, but it's more money), is pull your PCMCIA card out, plug your Voyager VGA card in, and plug the VGA monitor into its serial port just as if you were plugging it into the serial port of your laptop. This is cool stuff . . . and more importantly, you're going to save on chiropractic bills because instead of lugging an eight-pound laptop around, now all you've got to carry is your one-pound iPAQ.

Try This:
Tips for Running PowerPoint
Presentations on Mobile Devices

- Insert a blank slide as the first slide. This decreases the index needed on your presentation and will make the file smaller, therefore run faster.

- Invest in some Compact Flash memory. You can use it like a hard drive and save presentations to the CF memory, freeing up the memory on your device. You just carry these around like disks or CDs.

- Try to keep presentations less than 8 MG. Usually this limit comes into play on your graphics card.

- Eliminate the transitions between slides. Transitions can make your file unnecessarily big.

- When running iPresenter with the Compaq Flash Card (aka things the documentation won't tell you):

- Close all other programs running on the iPAQ to increase speed.

- Run the Voyager (or other card) program first to set the resolution of the presentation. This is also called the Video Mode and will determine how sharply your image projects.

- Be sure to "Close VGA" in the card program, otherwise your presentation won't project onto the screen. Click OK to close this window.

- Open the Presentation Player and choose your presentation; select "tools" and then "VGA option" and then "VGA Presentation Mode."

Multi-Point Video/Audio

The human interaction part of web conferencing certainly plays an integral role in the adoption of the technology. While it is possible today to have multi-point video that allows you to see multiple participants in the web conference, allowing everyone to talk at the same time is still a technological challenge. It won't be long before we can have both video and audio streaming in from all conference participants, in effect, allowing for an almost face-to-face experience. So we'll all be able to have multiple conversations at the same time and talk across the virtual conference table.

The ability to be able to do this will increase the effectiveness of web conferences. Here's a real-world example. Imagine having a web conference with a team of hospital specialists discussing their experience or recommendations for a particular case on of the doctors has seen. Not only will this technology allow for knowledge exchange to happen with people who might not have had any other way to do so, but it could give needed insight into a particular problem.

This type of technology could play an important role in the new world in which we live. It could provide possibly life-saving feedback to teams of hospital administrators who are dealing with a large-scale emergency. Having a web conference could provide the needed direction from other hospitals that might be dealing with, or have dealt with, a similar situation. There aren't many other technologies besides web conferencing that would allow the interaction necessary under these dire circumstances.

Being able to do multi-point video and audio together will be a major breakthrough in the web conferencing market. In fact, this alone might be one factor that causes web conferencing to take off with the masses. The host of applications made possible will be limitless.

Complex Media Types

Once upon a time there was just a text file. Then there was the need for other types of files. And so the long path began of our need (and want) for more feature-rich, exciting media types. These include video and audio files as well as one-click integration with applications we might already be familiar with like email or e-calendaring packages. Using complex media types that will deliver advanced communications functionality across new devices that come onto the market will be the next wave. This will bring into play technological advances that we've already mentioned, like compression technology and high-speed communication delivery formats. Putting all of these pieces of the puzzle together will allow for the sharing of what we'll call "rich content" as part of presentations and/or web conference. Using these types of communications will make it more compelling for businesses to communicate with their customers, not just business-to-business activities, which is primarily where we see web conferencing being used now.

While many see web conferencing as a business application, in fact it is a business communication. As the support of media types becomes more prolific, we'll see web conferencing simply as *the* means for communication.

The types of communications that will take place will increase the ability of businesses to deal with their customers. Examples of this include troubleshooting or diagnosing problems at a customer's site. Using web conferencing that allows for data to be retrieved from a client's device (whatever that device might be), and then having a support center interact with that customer will increase the satisfaction of the customer. It will certainly be easier, from a customer's point of view, to deal with a support center in this manner if they can effectively correct your problem without you having to wait on hold on a phone line for a half-hour. Think of the possibilities if a support center can access your device, diagnosis the problem, and then correct it with a software patch that is downloaded to your device, all while on a web conference.

Closing the Gap Between the Haves and the Have-Nots

One of the most interesting social interactions with technology is deciding what equipment you need to do your job, or what is just cool to enjoy the capabilities of the technology. Many sophisticated technologies require an investment, not only in terms of time and energy on the user's part, but also from one's wallet. These investments certainly can limit the adoption of the technology and possibly the usefulness of it. Take the original video conferencing proposition for example. As a company, you had to commit substantial resources to configure, set up, and use a video conferencing system. While video conferencing opened the doors to some of the ideas we see taking shape today, the cost and complexity of deployment of the technology was a significant barrier to its general adoption. This presented a dilemma between the haves (those companies that had deep enough wallets to use the technology) and the have-nots (those that probably could have made use of the technology if only they could have afforded it).

The other side of this coin, or what happens when people get hold of a potentially cool idea and they can actually access it easily and afford it, can be seen in the explosion of instant messaging (IM) and chat rooms. The barrier to entry for using IM and/or video chat was all but eliminated due to the commonplace use of just an Internet connection. Regardless of what speed your connection is, it is possible to use these technologies.

Using instant messaging or online chats, the interaction one has with others is not as sophisticated as the web conferencing technologies we've talked about throughout this book; however, they can still influence human interaction in a profound way. It becomes possible to have effective, or just fun, interaction with people who might be thousands of miles away. This is phenomenal. When ease of use met affordability, the Internet as a substitute for the telephone took off. Imagine what will happen when ease of use meets affordability with web conferencing, using rich media content at real-time speed? It will be then that the ways that we adjust our methods of communication, yet still produce outcomes similar to in-person interactions, will seriously emerge.

Our point is that it will happen because, as demonstrated by instant messaging and chat rooms, it's happened before.

So Here We Are

Web conferencing has the potential to completely change the way we look at human interactions. It can eliminate the barriers to entry for a whole host of new businesses and individuals. The cost of entry will continue to drop until the use of web conferencing is ubiquitous in our Internet lives. When this happens, we'll see an absolute explosion of the uses of web conferencing in ways that we can't imagine right now. But we're working on it.

We will all be watching closely, or better yet will be involved with the emergence of solutions and technology in this fascinating field. There are many areas (like the ones we've discussed) that will see all sorts of new ideas coming forward. If we allow ourselves the experience of interacting on a new level, we should all see some pretty amazing applications and solutions take shape. It is all about ease of use and ease of access and those days are not that far away.

Appendix A

Assessment Tool

An assessment tool, regardless how it is administered, can go a very long way in ensuring that you select the best web conferencing strategy for your business—a strategy that will be embraced and used to its fullest by members of your team or organization.

You can administer the tool as a questionnaire over your intranet, on paper, or verbally through focus groups in which the responses are being recorded by one means or another. You may also choose to pilot one of the web conferencing products we've featured or another of your choosing by creating a PowerPoint presentation about the merits of the strategy and getting feedback on the assessment via the polling, Q&A, chat, or test mechanisms that come standard in most web conferencing packages. The medium you choose will determine how you set up the assessment tool.

We have identified four assessment areas and have listed the pertinent questions under each. The more widely you can distribute the assessment tool, the more valuable will be its results. For the first three, you should attempt to get people from every level and every part of your organization to respond. The more input you get, the better your resulting implementation of the technology is bound to be. The last area, product capabilities, includes questions you should ask yourself about the products you are considering.

1. *Business Case*
   - Can you paraphrase, in five sentences or less, the goals and objectives of your organization?
   - Can you paraphrase, in three sentences or less, the strategy(ies) most important in helping you achieve the goals and objectives of your organization?
   - How do you define "technology" as applied to your functional area in the organization?
   - What do you think the annual expenditure is for this technology in your functional area, and do you think that amount is appropriate? If yes, why? If no, why?
   - In general, do you think that technology as you define it is an appropriate means by which the organization can achieve its business goals and objectives?

2. *Implementation Planning*
   - If there were one or two type of technology that you could get immediately to help you do your job better, what would they be?
   - Do you have the right tools available to you now to communicate and collaborate freely and effectively with others?
   - If there were just one thing that you could get to help you communicate better with others internal and external to the organization, what would it be?
   - Do you think that only IT (Information Technology) personnel should be involved in the selection and roll-out of new technology for the organization?
   - If your answer to the above question was some form of "no," who in your organization/department/team do you believe would be the best individual to participate in the planning for new technology?
   - What is your personal understanding of web conferencing and what it can do?

- If the organization were to invest in web conferencing as you understand it, do you think it would be valuable to you in doing your job? Why or why not?

- If you don't think web conferencing would be valuable to you in your function, are there any functional areas of the organization where you do think it would be valuable? If so, which and why?

- If you did have access to web conferencing, which of the following capabilities do you think would be most important to you: the ability to share data resident on your desktop; the ability to see others or have them see you via a PC camera; or the ability to be able to speak to them regardless of whether data or video were also transmitted?

- If you did have access to web conferencing at your desktop, what do you think you'd use it for? (Put down many uses as you can think of.)

- Do you personally, typically resist new technology in any aspect of your life? Why or why not?

- If you have resisted new technology in the workplace in the past, did you come to embrace it after a while? Why or why not?

- Do you know who, in your physical workplace, is accountable to you now for the technology you use to do your job?

- Do you think new technology should be rolled out and implemented all at once, or in phases across the organization?

3. *Education and Communications*

   - How important is it to you that senior management/administration (whom you might not interact with regularly on any other basis) be personally involved in the roll-out and communications of new technologies in the organization?

   - Do you prefer to learn about new technology that you can use to do your job:

     - In a classroom with others who are at your same level of knowledge about it?

- In your own working environment with a small group of people getting instruction?

- One-on-one with an expert?

- Via a book or manual assuming you're given focused time to read the documentation and use the tool?

- By simply being thrown into the deep end of the pool and learning it by using it?

4 *Product Capabilities* (Questions to ask yourself about the products you are considering):[1]

- Will the product support all of the client platforms you use?

- Does it absolutely require Windows, or if it runs on other operating systems, are there limitations?

- What are the vendor's browser, hardware, and operating system requirements for maximum performance?

- Does the product include the tools that your people will want to use like chat, whiteboarding, desktop sharing, web surfing, and so on.

- Does the product include integrated teleconferencing and/or VOIP? Is this important to you?

- Do you need video? If so, do you know exactly why?

- Does the product integrate with groupware applications that you will continue to use?

- Does the product allow for company branding?

- What are the levels/strategies for security in the product and are they sufficient for your proposed utilization?

- If you are anticipating growth of your organization, will the product easily scale to accommodate it?

Note

1. *eWeek* (July 1, 2002), p. 37.

Resources

Consulting Resource

For assistance regarding web conferencing software, online meeting content, and training delivery and design, contact Sue Spielman and Liz Winfeld of Switchback Software LLC at www.switchbacksoftware.com.

NOTE: A search on a search engine like Google or Yahoo under applicable keywords like "netmeeting," "PC cameras," "online training," "audio conferencing," "telephone," and so on will yield literally hundreds, if not thousands of links. What follows are a few that we identified as being valuable places to start.

Information Clearinghouses

NOTE: Some of the information/services provided on these sites is downloadable for free, but some of it requires that you purchase a subscription to the service as is common with analyst organizations.

1. www.conferzone.com. A very detailed site about audio, video, and web conferencing.

2. www.wainhouse.com. An analyst organization focused on conferencing technology. You can sign up for email notices of bulletins, conferences, and other news-oriented services that they provide.

3. www.frost.com. Similar to Wainhouse. Sometimes it's a good idea to see or hear what more than one analyst is saying.

Home Use Resources

1. http://www.netmeetinghq.com. Everything NetMeeting, including the NetMeeting Resource Kit, downloads of latest software and fixes, lists of MID and ILS servers, chat rooms, and more.

2. www.meetingbywire.com. Meeting by Wire is a service providing information, tips, and rumors about products that support distance meetings and conferences.

3. www.ofoto.com. An off-shoot of Kodak, Ofoto is an online photo print service that offers advanced editing capabilities and the tools to create things like greeting cards, posters, photo albums, calendars, and software to help you get your digital pictures edited and readied for printing in hard copy either on your own printer or by sending it in electronically.

4. www.intel.com. For online information about Intel's Create & Share software and PC cameras,

5. www.logitech.com. A big name in home PC accessories.

6. www.ibm.com. Perhaps you've heard of them? Yes, they make this stuff too.

7. www.amazon.com. In their electronics/computer add-ons pages, you will find a great representation of the major PC camera vendors, their features, and products.

Telephony

1. www.att.com. A good place to start if you want to explore all of the semantics of audio conferencing before you dive in somewhere.

2. www.acttel.com. Audio conferencing provider, as mentioned in Chapter 6.

3. www.voyant.com. audio conferencing provider, as mentioned in Chapter 6.

4. http://www.cconvergence.com. Offering a site called Comm Web. The site has a lot of very technical specification-type infor-

mation on it, which isn't always a bad thing. But it also has a Buyer's Guide section that can be very helpful.

5. http://www.tmcnet.com/it.   Internet Telephony Magazine's website. Nuf said.

Vendor Sites (listed in the order they appear in this book):

1. www.webex.com

2. www.interwise.com

3. www.eroom.com

4. www.genesis.com

5. www.centra.com

6. www.workworlds.com

7. www.placeware.com

8. www.intercall.com

9. www.spartacom.com (for Linktivity products)

And here are some others you might want to explore:

10. www.groove.com

11. www.raindance.com

12. www.latitude.com

Pricing Models for Web Conferencing Software

We hesitate to quote actual pricing from the vendors we've covered in this book, or any other for that matter, because chances are the dollar amounts for their services will have changed by the time we go to press. So please be advised that the figures we use in the following explanations are averages (as of the end of 2002) of the cost of various types of pricing models. We provide this information just to give you an idea—there is no promise or implication that these are the actual prices you will find.

We identified seven different pricing options:

1. Monthly subscription: These subscriptions will be paid monthly and the cost will depend on how many users (named individuals) or seats (nodes on your network) are signed on to the service. Estimated cost is $80 per seat or user.

2. Per server/per user licenses: A per server fee will run around $15,000 to $17,000 annually with about a $200 to $300 annual per user fee.

3. Concurrent users per month: In concurrent user models, there will be unlimited access to whatever data, audio, and video capabilities there are in the software, and the pricing tends to be tiered so that the more concurrent licenses you buy, the less each license is on a per monthly basis. For example, a fifteen-user concurrent license might be $150/user per month; a sixteen to twenty-five person license would drop to $135/user per month; and a twenty-six to one hundred person license might be $115/user per month.

4. Annual fee (with or without setup fee): In this scheme, you pay an annual fee of around $80,000 for unlimited use of the software no matter the number of your people or where they are located. There may be a one-time setup fee that can be in excess of $15,000.

5. Leveled usage services: These refer to "Silver," "Gold," or "Platinum" programs that vendors may make available at different price points for enhanced services. An example of an enhanced service is the ability to "brand" your web conferencing interface to have the same look and feel as all of your other internal/external communications. Another example might be advanced recording capabilities or more sophisticated security capabilities.

6. Per seat: Per seat is the first of the al la carté pricing options. Although similar to concurrent user pricing models, per set pricing is different because it will be the same regardless of how many users are involved (so no tiers are involved) and most everything associated with the use of the product will come at an additional cost. So, for example, if you want video or VOIP or branding or enhanced security, you can get them. But you'll pay for them on an as-needed basis instead of across the board. About $100 per seat as a base price (monthly) would be in the ballpark.

7. Per minute—pay per use: And this would be the second of the al la carté models. Here, you are paying for everything, including the actual time you spend on a web conferencing, as you use it. This is, frankly, a mechanism best used by small organizations who are not using the technology a lot (yet), or by home users who'd like to participate in web conferencing using a tool that has a bit more horsepower than NetMeeting. Prices typically range from 39 cents

to 45 cents per minute and these services can also, usually be charged to a credit card. You can even set up a credit charge account for that purpose with some web conferencing vendors.

In so far as conference call services are concerned, pricing can follow any one of the following (similar to the earlier) models:

1. Per minute/no contract/no fees: In this model, you can connect usually up to about one hundred different people at a time from anywhere, to anywhere and you will pay a per minute fee regardless of who's calling in and from where. It is not unusual in this model to find a different per minute rate for domestic calls as opposed to international calls, although you can have both domestic and international participation on a given call.

2. A monthly subscription: As earlier, you pay a monthly fee to access a conferencing service. The charge can be by number of users, by types of service, or by what types of service is used by different users.

INDEX